Matthew Morrison

Big Questions

Incredible Adventures in Thinking

Wizard Books

Published in the UK in 2007 by Wizard Books,
an imprint of Icon Books Ltd., The Old Dairy,
Brook Road, Thriplow, Cambridge SG8 7RG
email: wizard@iconbooks.co.uk
www.iconbooks.co.uk/wizard

Sold in the UK, Europe, South Africa and Asia by
Faber and Faber Ltd., 3 Queen Square, London WC1N 3AU
or their agents

Distributed in the UK, Europe, South Africa and Asia by
TBS Ltd., TBS Distribution Centre, Colchester Road,
Frating Green, Colchester CO7 7DW

Published in Australia in 2007 by
Allen & Unwin Pty. Ltd., PO Box 8500,
83 Alexander Street, Crows Nest, NSW 2065

Distributed in Canada by Penguin Books Canada,
90 Eglinton Avenue East, Suite 700,
Toronto, Ontario M4P 2Y3

ISBN-10: 1-84046-670-7
ISBN-13: 978-1840466-70-6

Typesetting by Wayzgoose

Printed in the UK by CPI Bookmarque, Croydon CR0 4TD

For my family

Contents

Introduction

In 399 BCE, a man named Socrates was sentenced to death in the Ancient Greek city of Athens. His only crime had been to encourage people to think for themselves and ask important questions about the world around them.

At the time, the rulers of Athens preferred citizens to do what they were told and not ask too many questions. They worried that Socrates was spreading rebellious ideas about how the government should be run. They warned him to stop, and when he refused, they forced him to drink the juice of the deadly plant hemlock.

Throughout his life, Socrates had been an inspirational teacher. He wanted to understand everything he could about our lives and loved talking about art and religion as well as politics and justice. Far from stopping the discussion of his ideas, his death encouraged his friends and pupils to examine them more closely. One in particular, a brilliant student named **Plato**, had already opened a school dedicated to exploring the questions Socrates had raised. It was here, almost 2,500 years ago, that the study of philosophy began. (The word itself comes from a Greek phrase meaning a love of wisdom or knowledge.)

★

Without knowing it, you've probably already asked yourself all sorts of philosophical questions. For example, have you ever wondered how you can be sure the world around you actually exists? Everything *seems* real enough, but isn't it possible that it's all a figment of your imagination? Perhaps you're just experiencing a very vivid dream, one which you'll wake from any minute?

This is the kind of intriguing problem that philosophers love. That's because, ever since Socrates' time, they've tried to find the truth about the universe and our place within it. They're not afraid to ask strange and surprising questions in order to get to the bottom of things.

Big Questions is an introduction to some of the most fascinating puzzles in philosophy, such as: 'Is there a reason for everything?' 'Do animals have the same rights as people?' 'Why do we have governments?' and 'Does God exist?'

Each chapter begins with apparently simple, everyday problems before looking at some of the most entertaining and mind-bending questions of all. Along the way, we'll meet some of the most brilliant philosophers in history, and pick up some useful tips on how to win arguments with your friends! Extra information on words or phrases that appear in bold can be found at the back of the book.

With sections including *Minds and Bodies*, *God and Nature* and *Right and Wrong*, this book takes you on an extraordinary journey where nothing is quite what you expect!

Truth and Knowledge

How much do you know?

Have you ever asked yourself how many things you know? If you tried to write a list, you'd probably never get to the end.

For starters, you know all sorts of things about yourself. You know your name and where you live. You know what you look like. You know the colour of your eyes and the colour of your skin.

And as well as facts about yourself, you also know countless things about the world you live in. You ought to know that the earth is round. You may also know that water covers over 70 per cent of its surface. You know that apples can be green or red. You probably didn't know that there are over 2,000 different varieties in the UK alone. If you're interested in geography you might know that Africa is the largest continent and that the Nile is the longest river in the world – 4,145 miles to be precise. You might not know that the shortest river measures only 37 metres. You know that we are living in the 21st century. If you're interested in history you might know that the First World War broke out in 1914, or that the French Revolution began in 1789.

But how do we actually come to have this knowledge, and can we ever be 100 per cent sure we haven't made a mistake? These are questions that have fascinated philosophers for thousands of years. We can start to answer them by looking at what it really means to say we *know* something.

Throughout this section, we'll be using the word **statement** quite a bit. A statement is just a particular type of sentence – one that says something is the case. So, for example, 'giraffes have long necks' is a statement because it says something about giraffes. 'Bananas are yellow' is a statement because it says something about bananas. Both these statements happen to be true, but statements can be false too. The statement 'all cats are blue' says something about cats. It just so happens that it's nonsense. As we'll see, statements are either true or false.

Three steps to knowledge

One of the first people who questioned how we know things was the Greek philosopher **Plato**. He thought that to have knowledge of something we had to tick three different boxes: belief; good reason; and truth. Let's have a look at these in turn.

Step 1: Belief

To really know something, argued Plato, we have to believe it too. It wouldn't make much sense to say, 'I know the earth is round, but I don't believe it is.' On the other hand, if you know that cats have four legs, you're bound to believe it as well.

But Plato doesn't mean that belief and knowledge are the same thing. After all, history is full of mistaken beliefs. Here are some big ones …

Walking on fire

Some of the very first philosophers believed the world was made up of a single substance like air or water. Heraclitus, an ancient Greek philosopher, even suggested that fire was the basis of everything.

Going round the world

During the 17th century, many people still believed that the sun travelled around the Earth, rather than the other way around. When the astronomer and physicist Galileo challenged this belief, the Roman Catholic Church arrested him.

A nice pint of blood

For hundreds of years, doctors thought that blood-letting was the most effective cure for disease. Up to two pints of blood would be drained from the body, often several times a day, to remove the source of infection. Needless to say, the treatment did more harm than good. Unfortunate patients were actually being bled to death!

Plato recognised that beliefs could often be mistaken. A belief isn't enough *on its own* to give you knowledge, but it was one of the three necessary elements.

The medical condition known as blindsight provides an interesting challenge to Plato's idea. Sufferers of this condition are unable to see objects placed in front of them. However, when asked to guess if there's actually something there or not, they usually answer correctly. It's as if they see the object without realising it. They know something's there, even if they don't believe they do!

Step 2: Having a good reason

In a general knowledge quiz, John is asked: What's the tallest mountain in Wales?

A) Mount Snowdon.

B) Mount Etna.

C) Mountbatten.

John really has no idea, but he's got a weird feeling that the answer might be 'A'. Luckily, he's right. Mount Snowdon *is* the tallest Welsh mountain, standing at 1085 metres above sea level.

It turned out that the answer John gave was true. But his belief that he'd be right was based on nothing more than a 'weird feeling'. It doesn't seem fair to say he knew the answer, when it was really just a lucky guess.

According to Plato, for a belief to count as knowledge, it must also be backed up by good reasons.

(Mount Etna is an extremely active volcano in Sicily. Mountbatten isn't a mountain at all. He was an English Lord who became Governor General of India in 1947.)

Step 3: Telling the truth

The third of Plato's requirements is that the belief you have must definitely be true. It's not enough to *believe* that 70 per cent of our planet is covered by water. To really *know* that fact, it actually has to be the case.

Let's look at things the other way round. You couldn't *know* that the Earth was made of fire, however much you believed it, because the Earth just isn't made of fire.

Or to take another example, you might *believe* that blood-letting is perfectly sensible – you might even think you had good reasons for your belief – but you couldn't actually *know* it, because blood-letting is really very bad for you.

Remember that in each of these examples we're concerned with whether a particular statement is true or false. As we've seen, statements are sentences that say something is the case. And we tend to think that statements are true if they match the way the world really is. The statement 'That shark has very big teeth' will be true if you happen to be swimming beside a shark with very big teeth. The statement 'There was a snow storm this morning' will be false if you're in the middle of a heat wave.

So to sum up, these are the three things we need in order to have knowledge:

1. We need to *believe* a certain statement.

2. We need to have *good reasons* for our belief.

3. The statement has to be *true* (which is to say that it has to match something in the world).

Now try thinking back to some of the things you feel you already know. How many of them would pass Plato's tests?

And when you've done that, you can test yourself on the rest of John's quiz …

The Knowledge Quiz

1. What is the world's most poisonous creature?

A) Golden poison frog
B) Gall wasp
C) Black widow spider

2. True or false, a cockroach can live for a week without its head?

A) True
B) False

3. What is the world's driest desert?

A) Sahara
B) Gobi
C) Antarctica

4. Who is the richest person in the world?

A) The Queen of England
B) Bill Gates, founder of Microsoft Computers
C) Britney Spears

5. What is the smallest mammal in the world?

A) A bat
B) A mouse
C) A squirrel

6. What is the world's fastest animal?

A) Cheetah
B) Python
C) Peregrine Falcon

7. True or false, every human being's tongue print is identical?

A) True
B) False

8. In the time it takes to read this sentence, how many of your body's cells will have died and been replaced?

A) Approximately 50
B) Approximately 5,000
C) Approximately 50,000

9. What is the world's most deadly disease?

A) Heart disease
B) Cancer
C) Common cold

10. True or false, no piece of paper can be folded in half more than seven times?

A) True
B) False

Answers

1. A: Just 1 mg of poison from this frog would be enough to kill 10–20 human beings.
2. A: A cockroach's brain is actually distributed around its body, so cutting off the head won't kill it at once. However, cockroaches do need their heads to eat and drink. A headless cockroach will eventually die of thirst or starvation.
3. C: Despite being covered in ice, Antarctica has the least annual rainfall of any desert.
4. B.
5. A: The bat in question is the Kitti's hog-nosed bat at only 3 cm long.
6. C: A peregrine falcon in a dive can reach speeds of over 300 kph.
7. B. Like a fingerprint, every single human tongue has a unique pattern.
8. C.
9. A: Heart disease kills about 7 million people a year.
10. A: Why don't you try it?

★

Plato thought he'd cracked what it means to know something 100 per cent. But have a read of these next two examples. Things may not be as straightforward as he thought ...

Beware of the bull

One afternoon, Alan and Jack are walking in the countryside. Hopping over a stile into a field they suddenly notice a very large animal moving slowly towards them.

'Oh look,' says Alan, 'what a lovely cow.'

'That's not a cow,' replies Jack, nervously. 'It's a bull.'

'No, I'm pretty sure it's just a cow,' says Alan as he begins to stride across the field. The animal snorts and quickens its pace towards them.

'It's definitely a bull.' whispers Jack. 'I know it's a bull because I used to work on a farm. I've seen hundreds of bulls. That animal has horns, like a bull and there is a big sign over there that says "Beware of the bull". Now, RUN!!!'

'Sorry about that,' says Alan when the two friends have finally stopped running. 'I really thought it was a cow. I've never seen a bull before and I didn't spot the sign. Lucky you were here, really.'

Both Alan and Jack thought they knew what the animal in front of them was. Both of them had reasons for backing up their claim, but only Jack's were convincing. What's more, his belief was actually true. So it seems fair to say that Jack *knew* there was a bull in the field, and Plato's three boxes have been ticked.

But the next day, things get a little bit more complicated ...

Beware of the cow

It's a lovely sunny morning and Alan and his dad happen to be driving past the very same field.

'There's a bull over there,' says Alan, shuddering at the thought.

'How do you know?' replies his dad, who's too busy watching the road to notice.

'Well I can see it, for one thing,' says Alan, squinting in the sunlight. 'There's also a sign saying "Beware of the bull" and yesterday the thing tried to kill me.'

Like Jack the day before, Alan seems to have pretty good reasons for his belief. And there is indeed a bull in the field. The only problem is it's not the animal that Alan's pointing to.

In fact, the bull that charged at him is lurking quietly behind a hedge. The creature that Alan can see in the distance is actually a very peaceful cow.

It seems that something's gone wrong with our three tests. Alan believes there's a bull in the field, he has good reasons for that belief (his eyes and his recent experience) and there is actually a bull there somewhere. So why doesn't it seem quite right to say that Alan knew the bull was there?

Perhaps the problem is simply that Alan didn't have all the information needed to come to the right conclusion. He thought he had good reasons for his belief, but actually they weren't quite good enough.

But how are we ever supposed to know that our reasons are good enough? Even when we think we've all the evidence we need, it's always possible we've missed something along the way.

Thinking back to blood-letting, doctors probably had perfectly sensible reasons for believing it was a good idea, given what they knew at the time. It's natural to think we know much more about medicine and science now, but perhaps the reasons we have for some of our firmly held beliefs will also turn out to be mistaken in the future.

The truth at last

In the middle of all this uncertainty, you might be relieved to know there are some things we can know for sure.

Here's an example of a statement that simply *must* be true.

'All black cats are black.'

There are two things that everybody knows about black cats: (1) they're black and (2) they're cats. So this statement isn't telling us anything very surprising. Indeed, it's telling us something blindingly obvious. But maybe that's what makes it true. It's so obvious, it couldn't possibly be false.

If you're not convinced, try imagining the statement was false after all. That would mean that 'all black cats are *not* black' or maybe just '*not* all black cats are black'. Surely that would be nonsense?

In fact, you could tell the statement was true even if you'd never seen a black cat in real life. You can tell just by looking at the words.

Philosophers call statements that can be seen to be true just by examining, or analysing, them *analytically* true.

The problem with these **analytic statements** is that they don't give us very useful information about the world. On the other hand, a statement like 'Huge sea monsters exist in Scotland', might be extremely useful …

Does the Loch Ness Monster exist?

Scientists Dr McDonald and Dr Islan are fascinated by the legend of Nessie – the prehistoric creature said to lurk beneath the surface of Loch Ness. Dr McDonald, persuaded by eyewitness reports, is sure the animal exists. Dr Islan, on the other hand, believes the whole thing's an elaborate hoax. So together they hire some extremely expensive under-water equipment to try to settle the question.

For a month they search Loch Ness in vain and at last Dr Islan declares victory. 'Now I *know* that the creature doesn't exist.'

Dr McDonald doesn't think his colleague knows anything of the sort. Loch Ness is 24 miles long, over a mile wide and 750 feet deep in places. They couldn't possibly have covered every bit of it. There are bound to be scores of hidden under-water caves left to explore. And anyway, their equipment may have been unreliable, not to mention their own eyesight. 'Admit it,' he argues, 'you can't be 100 per cent certain that the creature doesn't exist. However unlikely it is, it's still possible that it does.'

Nessie update: In 1987, 20 boats carrying hi-tech sonar equipment searched Loch Ness unsuccessfully for signs of the monster. But even the thoroughness of this investigation failed to satisfy everyone that the creature wasn't real.

The problem of knowledge

Philosophers and scientists find themselves in a frustrat-ing situation. Statements that *have* to be true, such as 'All four-legged dogs have four legs', don't tell us any-thing useful or surprising about the world.

On the other hand, statements that do give helpful information, such as 'All spiders eat flies', might be true or false. Even if you never came across a single spider that didn't eat flies in your whole life, one might, just possibly, exist somewhere.

Can you be sure?

People who think we can never be 100 per cent sure about anything are called **sceptics**. They believe everything's open to doubt because our five senses (sight, smell, taste, touch and hearing) are so unreliable. They have plenty of examples to illustrate their point:

Mirages: In the desert, people desperate for thirst often imagine they see water, when really there's nothing ahead but sand.

Weird perspective: Try putting a stick into a glass of water. Looked at from a certain angle, the stick will appear bent, even though you know it's perfectly straight.

Bad taste: Have you ever had a fizzy drink after brushing your teeth? Doesn't it taste totally different to normal?

Bumpy surface: A table-top might seem smooth to the naked eye, but under a microscope it can look like a mountain range.

According to sceptics, we are constantly being misled about what the world is really like. How can we ever be certain of anything, if we can't even trust our senses?

Perhaps the most famous sceptical argument was put forward by the French philosopher **Rene Descartes**. He raised the possibility that everything we think we know is just the result of God playing tricks on us. We'll look at this idea in more detail in a later chapter (*Minds and Bodies*). In the meantime, watch out for other sceptical arguments that might crop up. And be careful. Although they often seem far-fetched, proving them wrong can be harder than you think.

Arguments (and how to win them!)

In philosophy, an argument doesn't just mean a shouting match between people with different opinions. Not that philosophers are above that kind of thing. In 1946, **Ludwig Wittgenstein** got into such a fiery debate with fellow thinker Karl Popper he attacked him with a red-hot poker!

But the word has another meaning, too. Philosophical arguments can be described as a way of setting out ideas very clearly and precisely. Arguments, in this sense of the word, help philosophers explain why they believe certain things. For instance, if a philosopher wanted to convince you that God existed, he or she would set out an argument to try and *prove* it.

Philosophical arguments often have several steps, or stages, and need to be followed carefully. The best arguments are hard to disagree with because each individual step makes good sense and leads on naturally from the one before. Bad arguments may seem OK at first, but look closely and they are full of holes.

Bad arguments are often used deliberately to convince people of strange and misleading things. (This is the sort of devious behaviour that politicians get accused of!) It's easy to trick someone with a clever argument – something that looks reasonable on the surface but turns out to be rather suspect underneath.

This chapter is about what makes a good argument. And it's also about spotting when someone's pulling the wool over your eyes. We'll start off by looking at four well-known examples:

1. Slippery slopes.

2. Dodgy comparisons.

3. Either/or problems.

4. Syllogisms.

Then we'll look at a few extra tips to help you become a seriously sharp thinker. Next time you're in a disagreement with someone, you'll be sure to come off best!

A slippery slope

Slippery slope arguments are just the sort of thing people like to use on their children. As with most arguments, they have several steps. Perhaps you can imagine one of your parents coming up with the following example:

Step 1: If you don't brush your teeth today, they'll start to rot.

Step 2: Pretty soon they'll all fall out.

Step 3: Then you won't be able to eat.

Step 4: And it won't be long before you starve to death.

You can probably see how this type of argument got its name. Once you take the first step down a particular slope, you'll quickly slide all the way to the bottom. In arguments like this, the first step starts a chain of events that almost always ends in disaster.

But when we look more closely, we can see that downhill slides are rarely as unstoppable as they appear. The example above makes it look like failing to brush your teeth, even once, will inevitably lead to tragedy. In fact, you'd probably be fine as long as you took better care in the future. And even if your teeth did fall out one day, you could still get false ones fitted, or eat porridge for the rest of your life. In any case, it's unlikely you'd end up starving to death. The problem with the argument is that each step looks like it follows naturally from the one before. Actually, that isn't true at all.

Politicians and newspapers use arguments like this all the time. Here's an example that might seem familiar:

'If we let foreigners into this country they'll take all our jobs, kick us out of our homes and soon the country will go to the dogs.'

The next time you hear something like this, you might want to think twice about it. Slippery slope arguments grab our attention, and if we're not thinking clearly, it's easy to be swept along. But take a moment to consider them, and you'll often see that one step doesn't necessarily lead to another.

Dodgy comparisons

Another type of argument that's worth watching out for is based on comparing things that seem similar, but are actually very different. Here's an example:

Breaking the rules ...

When Jamelia fails to hand in her homework one day, her teacher, Mrs Patel, threatens to call the police.

Jamelia thinks she must be joking, but Mrs Patel is deadly serious. 'Rules are there to be obeyed,' she barks. 'When criminals break the law – the *rules* of society – they're put in prison. You've broken the school rules and will be treated the same.'

When people use comparisons in this way, their arguments can seem convincing. But the ways in which things are different are as important as the ways in which they're the same.

If you think hard enough, similarities can be found almost anywhere. You might say that a cat is like a table because they both have four legs. But just because you can find one thing in common doesn't prove much by itself. Schools and governments both lay down rules, but breaking them shouldn't require the same punishments. After all, running in the corridor is very different to robbing a bank.

Here's another dodgy comparison. Like many arguments, it is set out step by step.

Step 1: Guns are banned in this country because they can be used to kill people.

Step 2: But rolling pins can be used to kill people too.

Step 3: Therefore rolling pins should also be banned.

This argument is based on something guns and rolling pins have in common. But although you probably could kill someone with a rolling pin, there are many more ways in which the two things are different. For one thing, guns are useless for making pastry.

So remember, if you're going to use comparisons in an argument, always consider the differences as well as the similarities between the things you are describing.

Dodgy jokes ...

Some comedians deliberately use unlikely comparisons to come up with jokes. They take two very different kinds of objects and try and find something that connects them. Mind you, the results aren't always that successful ...

Q: Why is a cat with a cold like a bag of rubbish?

A: They both smell badly.

(If you didn't find that hilarious, why don't you see if you can do better?)

Either/or

Slippery slopes and dodgy comparisons are pretty sneaky ways to win your case. Either/or arguments are also surprisingly common, but to spot them, you need to keep your wits about you. Here's an example that doesn't seem too controversial:

Either it's is raining *or* it's not raining.

This is a perfectly reasonable argument. The weather must be doing one of these two things, and it certainly can't be doing both at once. In fact, either/or arguments are absolutely fine, as long as there really are only two options to choose from. But take a look at the following sentence, which is clearly nonsense:

Either today is Wednesday *or* it's Saturday.

Needless to say, today doesn't have to be Wednesday or Saturday at all. It might be Monday or Friday or any other day of the week. Unfortunately, not all suspicious either/or arguments are quite so easily identified. Take this example:

> *Either* you vote for the Green Party *or* global warming will get worse.

Again, it looks as if there are only two alternatives. If we don't want global warming to get worse, we have no option but to vote Green. But in fact, there might be other political parties that also want to reduce global warming; we could vote for them instead. And it's possible that global warming will get worse even if the Green Party does get elected. Although the argument makes it seem like we only have two choices, several other possibilities are available. (We'll look at the issue of global warming again in the *Science and Scientists* section.)

Watch out for other suspect either/or arguments, particularly in advertising. They're often used to try and sell you things. For example, here's an ad for a new type of toothpaste:

> Brushing every day is the only way to protect your teeth.
> So buy DentoFix™, or they'll all fall out!

Again, it looks like we only have two options. *Either* we buy DentoFix, *or* we lose our teeth. But these aren't actually the only two options. For one thing, we could just choose to buy a different brand.

The perfect argument

Now that we're getting a feel for good and bad arguments, let's take a look at the most famous philosophical argument of all. Ancient Greeks called it the syllogism.

As we'll see, all syllogisms are made up of steps and a conclusion. The following example is designed to show that a crow has wings:

Step 1: All birds have wings.

Step 2: A crow is a type of bird.

Therefore: A crow has wings.

Notice that the first two steps of the argument are true, and the conclusion seems to follow on quite naturally. A crow has wings because, first, *all* birds have wings and, second, a crow is a type of bird.

All good syllogisms work in exactly the same way. Here's another example:

Step 1: All dogs bark.

Step 2: Buster is a dog.

Therefore: Buster barks.

Again, as long as you agree with the first two steps of the argument, you should also agree with the conclusion.

A suspicious twist

But here's where things get interesting. It's very easy to set out an argument that looks just like a syllogism, but isn't all it seems. Take a look at the following:

Step 1: All birds have wings.

Step 2: Otis has wings.

Therefore: Otis must be a bird.

At first glance this looks just like the previous example, but in fact, even if the first two sentences are true, it doesn't mean that Otis is a bird. That's because lots of animals have wings. It's possible that Otis is a bird, but he could also be a dragonfly, or a wasp or even a light aircraft.

The conclusion that Otis *must* be bird hasn't been proved at all.

Let's look at another example.

Step 1: *Only* birds have wings.

Step 2: Otis has wings.

Therefore: Otis is a bird.

That seems a bit better. If birds are the *only* things that have wings, and Otis has wings, then Otis must be a bird.

But that's a big 'if'. You don't have to be wildlife expert to know that birds are not the only creatures to have wings. The problem with this example is that step 1 just isn't true.

Make your own perfect argument

If you think you've got the hang of philosophical arguments, you might want to have a go at making your own. As it happens, there's a rather neat formula for creating syllogisms. Here it is:

Step 1: All (As) have (B).

Step 2: (C) is a type of (A).

Therefore: (C) will have (B).

Don't worry if this looks completely confusing! Just try replacing the letter (A) with any person or object you like. Now replace the letter (B) with any characteristic you like (dark hair, for example, or blue eyes). Finally replace the letter (C) with the name of a person, or animal or object. Now, as long as your first two steps are true, your conclusion will be true as well. Here's a final example to show you how it works.

Let's say: (A)= fox (B) = a bushy tail (C) = Fred

Replacing our letters with the words 'fox', 'bushy tail' and 'Fred' we get:

Step 1: Every fox has a bushy tail.

Step 2: Fred is a fox.

Therefore: Fred has a bushy tail.

Try making up your own syllogisms, and see if your friends can find anything wrong with them.

Good detective work

When you think hard about problems like these, you're really acting like a philosophical detective. Your job is to find the clues that show whether an argument is all it's cracked up to be. In the case of syllogisms, there are two big things to watch out for:

1. Does the conclusion actually follow from the first two steps?

2. Are those two steps actually true?

After those four examples, your brain might feel like it's spinning. Perhaps you've never used it in this way before, in which case you're already beginning to expand you mind. But before we finish with arguments for this chapter, here are a few extra tips that might come in useful ...

1. Don't go round in circles

When you're in an argument with someone, it's important that you both have the same definitions for the things you are discussing. Take the word 'cat', for example. Most people's definitions would include the facts that they're mammals, have four legs, like chasing mice etc.

Ben, however, happens to have the most useless dictionary in the world. In it, a cat is described as being 'a bit like a dog'. Worse still, when he looks up the definition of a dog, it just reads 'a bit like a cat'.

When words are defined in this way we say that the definitions are circular. Circular definitions don't tell us very much, so they're not much good in an argument.

Luckily Ben has a pretty good idea what the word 'cat' means. But when he tries to look up a much more unusual word – a word like 'philatelist' – he runs into bigger difficulties.

According to his dictionary, a 'philatelist' is defined as 'someone who practices philately'. 'Philately' on the other hand is described as 'something carried out by a philatelist'. After reading these two definitions, Ben is no closer to knowing what either 'philately' or a 'philatelist' might be. It's not that the definitions are inaccurate, just that they go round and round in circles.

In this book we'll see several examples of **circular arguments**. When we do, you might find it helpful to come back to the explanation in this section.

By the way, a 'philatelist' is actually someone who collects stamps. So 'philately' is just a big word for stamp collecting.

2. Ockham's razor

As we saw at the start of this chapter, philosophers use arguments to help explain their beliefs about the world. But sometimes it's difficult to show why one explanation is better than another. Have a look at Andy's dilemma in the following story:

Do you believe in ghosts?

Andy and Nicholas are brothers. And like most brothers, they often argue. For instance, Nicholas believes that ghosts tap on his bedroom window at night, keeping him awake. Andy doesn't believe in ghosts. He thinks his brother's just trying to scare him.

Andy explains that the tapping noises are just trees brushing against the windows in the wind. 'No,' insists Nicholas. 'There are ghosts out there. They've got long bony hands and fingernails like claws and they scratch at the window, trying to get in.'

One windy night Andy comes into his brother's bedroom and pulls back the curtains. 'Look,' he says. 'No ghosts.' Sure enough nothing can be seen except the silhouette of the branches pressing against the glass. This makes a fairly creepy sound, but there are certainly no ghosts to be seen.

'But there are ghosts,' says Nicholas, 'It's just, they're invisible. The branches do make some noise, but there are definitely ghosts out there too. You can't see them, but they tap on the window all the same. You can't prove I'm not telling the truth, so you might as well go back to your own bed-room and hope they don't come and get you in your sleep.'

Reluctantly, Andy gives up. He's sure his brother's talking nonsense, but he can't think of any way to *prove* him wrong.

Andy is pretty stuck. But even though he can't prove there aren't any ghosts, he can use a philosophical prin-ciple, or guiding rule, to show why his explanation is the best.

This principle goes by the unusual name of Ockham's Razor, having originally been suggested by a mediaeval monk called William of Ockham. The basic idea is that we shouldn't make explanations more complicated than they need to be. In other words, keep it simple. If there are two competing explanations for something, the simplest will probably be best. In the case of our ghost story, the tapping on the window-pane can be perfectly well explained by branches swaying in the wind. So there's no good reason to add extra explanations involving invisible ghosts.

This principle of Ockham's Razor remains one of philosophy's most helpful tools. Mind you, Ockham didn't always choose the best examples to illustrate his argument. For instance, he used his idea to dismiss the whole concept of movement. He thought it was simpler to believe that things just vanished and reappeared in new places! Philosophers have always had problems explaining how people get from one place to another. If you want to know why, skip to the Big Thinkers section and check out **Zeno of Elea**.

3. Choosing your words ...

When someone's trying to grab your attention, they'll usually choose their words very carefully. Journalists are particularly good at this. Consider these two headlines:

Heavy snowfall disrupts train service.

Blizzard causes rail chaos!

Both examples deal with the same fact, but the second is much more striking. The words 'blizzard' and 'chaos' create a more vivid impression than the phrases 'heavy snowfall' and 'train service'.

Politicians are also known for selecting their words precisely. The speech below is typical of the sort of argument they might use to try to persuade you of something:

Our brave soldiers are in terrible danger in Iraq. Many have been brutally slaughtered by enemy insurgents*. We must not allow any more mothers to

*An insurgent is someone who mounts an armed resistance to the established government.

lose their children. We must bring our troops home at once.

A bit of background: Whether Britain and America should withdraw their troops from Iraq has been a hotly debated issue. When they invaded the country in 2003 (with other European allies) it was to get rid of Saddam Hussein. This was controversial itself. Since the war ended, however, there have been violent clashes between different sections of society, particularly Shia and Sunni Muslims. Many Western politicians believe the Iraqi people resent having foreign soldiers in their country, and that this is making the problem worse. Others think the allied troops are needed to help protect Iraqis from the violence.

To make a decision for ourselves about these questions, we need to think very carefully about the facts. But the speech above is also deliberately appealing to our emotions. Notice how it mentions mothers losing their children. How does that make you feel? And what about phrases like 'brutally slaughtered' and 'terrible danger'? These are all examples of emotive language – words and phrases designed to make us react in a certain way. It's easy to be won over by arguments like this, but we need to make sure our emotional reaction doesn't stop us asking important questions about the information we're being given.

Here is another powerful example of emotive language. It's an extract from the speech made by US President George W. Bush following the terrorist attacks on the World Trade Centre in 2001. On that day (often known as 9/11) hijackers flew two passenger aeroplanes into the twin towers of the World Trade Centre in New York. Another plane was flown into the Pentagon in Washington and a fourth crashed near Pennsylvania. President Bush said:

> Great harm has been done to us. We have suffered great loss. And in our grief and anger we have found our mission and our moment. Freedom and fear are at war. The advance of human freedom, the great achievement of our time and the great hope of every time, now depends on us. Our nation, this generation, will lift a dark threat of violence from our people and our future. We will rally the world to this cause by our efforts, by our courage. We will not tire, we will not falter, and we will not fail.

The extract is extremely rousing. Notice how George Bush tries to encourage the American people to unite behind him with phrases like '*our* nation' and '*our* mission and moment'. The description of 'a dark threat of violence' is chilling, but with the final lines he tries to inspire his audience with strength and determination.

Another interesting discussion of emotive language centres around two possible descriptions of people prepared to use violence to achieve their goals: 'terrorist' and 'freedom fighter'. We'll look at this distinction in depth in the section on *Right and Wrong*. But for now, just make a note of your different emotional reaction to these two expressions.

4. Trusting the experts

When arguments are difficult to unravel by ourselves, it's tempting just to accept what we're told by people with greater experience. However, that doesn't always solve the problem. As Sarah and Jamelia are about to find out, the 'experts' don't always agree.

The best film ever

The two friends are at the cinema to see a new Hollywood blockbuster called 'Cogito!' It's based on the life of a famous French philosopher, and is supposed to be amazing. The quotes on the posters say it all: 'The best film of all time', 'A work of art!', 'The acting is magnificent', 'Awesome special effects'.

Sarah has only seen one newspaper review so far, but it's given the film eleven stars. Usually the ratings only go up to ten.

Two hours later they leave the cinema lost for words. 'Cogito!' was, without doubt, the worst film they've ever seen. The story was boring and predictable, the acting was wooden and Jamelia could have designed better effects on her computer at home. There's no way on earth that it was the best film of all time. And it certainly wasn't a work of art!

Then again, thinks Jamelia, each of those incredible comments on the poster was just an individual point of view. The reviewer in the paper was just one person too. Why should her opinion be any less important?

Sarah thinks differently. The reviewers are experts. They know when a film really is good or bad. This one must have been amazing like they said – she and Jamelia just aren't experienced enough to have realised it.

The two friends go home depressed and disappointed, but the next day several other newspapers publish their reviews. 'A complete flop,' declares one. 'Utter rubbish,' says another. 'A total waste of time,' says a third.

Jamelia thinks her friend will be delighted, but in fact she's even more upset than before. 'If even the experts can't agree on whether the film was any good,' she complains, 'how are we ever going to know the truth?'

The example above is an important reminder of why we need to make up our own minds, and not just trust the opinion of others. Experts might claim to have all the answers, but often they come up with completely different points of view. Surely they can't all be right.

So, just to recap, to keep your arguments razor sharp:

1. Don't go round in circles.

2. Remember Ockham's razor.

3. Choose your words carefully.

4. Don't rely on the experts.

Final thought

Over the centuries, people have searched for solutions to questions about the world we live in. But more recently, philosophers have begun to wonder if there really are any single right answers. Perhaps different ideas and beliefs don't have to contradict each other. Could it be that there are many different ways of looking at particular problems?

What do you see when you look at this picture?

Perhaps you can make out the outline of a duck's head. Or maybe it is easier to pick out the long ears of a hare. Perhaps you're able to switch between the different images. Neither interpretation is more acceptable, or 'right', than the other. There are just two different ways of viewing it.

Perhaps there are different, but equally acceptable, answers to many of the questions in this book.

Minds and Bodies

This chapter is about minds and bodies, and how they make us *who* we are.

Most of us think our bodies are made up of physical 'stuff' like skin and bones, muscles and tissues – things we could experience with our senses of smell, taste, touch, hearing and sight. For example, think about the way skin feels to touch, or the sound your fingers make if you click them.

On the other hand, we tend to think our minds are made up of non-physical stuff like thoughts and ideas, memories and emotions – things we can't actually experience with our five senses. You can't touch a memory, or smell a thought.

In the first part of this chapter we'll be asking how these different kinds of stuff make us the people we are. We'll be asking if we'd remain the same person if our bodies changed, or if we completely lost our minds.

★

Another big question, which we'll look at later in the chapter, concerns the way minds and bodies affect each other.

Have you ever gone bright red with embarrassment? Or hurt yourself by stubbing your toe? In both cases there's a connection between a physical change in your body (like blushing or bruising your foot) and a thought or feeling in your mind (like embarrassment or pain).

But exactly *how* your mind and body are connected is one of philosophy's biggest mysteries.

Who are you?

So, what is it that makes *you* the person that you are?

Next time you're on a crowded bus or train, have a good look at all the people around you. Why are you *you* and not one of the other passengers? What is it that makes you a one-off? Why are you unique?

One thing that makes you *you* is your body. A body with eyes and skin of a certain colour. A body that has a particular weight and height and moves in a certain way. A body that belongs to you and nobody else.

In fact, everyone's body is changing all the time, and sometimes those changes are very noticeable. In adolescence we are particularly aware of the way our bodies are developing. And throughout our lives, our cells continually die and are replaced, although the process is so gradual that we often don't realise it's happening.

But could your body change so much that you stopped being the same person altogether? How much change can a single body take?

A brand-new motor ...

Wendy buys a car from a dodgy used-car salesman and immediately things go wrong. The very first time she takes it for a drive, one of the doors falls off. The garage down the road fits a new one, but no sooner has Wendy driven away than the engine gives out. The mechanic replaces it and for about a week everything's fine. Until the brakes stop working. And another door falls off. And the nice retractable sun roof catches fire. Wendy's mechanic has his work cut out replacing all the things that go wrong and after a few weeks her car is made of completely new parts.

But if nothing of the original remains, is it really the same car she bought in the first place?

Imagine that parts of your body could be replaced in the same way? Surely if you lost a leg you'd still be the same person – even if you lost both legs and both your arms. And people can have liver, kidney and even face transplants. One day it might even be possible to have parts of your brain transplanted. Would you still be the same person after all these changes? What if a surgeon was able to take all the transplanted or removed pieces of your body and sew them back together? Which body would be yours – the one with completely new parts, or the old body that the surgeon has rebuilt?

The car **thought experiment** above raises the possibility that your entire body could be replaced without it changing who you really are. But if who we are doesn't depend on our bodies, what else might it depend on?

A good memory ...

On the opening night of actress Maria Lorez's latest film, a crowd gathers outside the cinema to catch a glimpse of the star arriving. As a huge white limousine rolls up, cameras flash and reporters surge forward. But the person who steps out onto the red carpet looks nothing like Maria Lorez. Everyone stands back and the cameras stop clicking. The woman is surprised. She calls to one of the reporters to see why he isn't asking any questions. When he explains who he's waiting for she hisses, 'But that's me, I'm Maria Lorez. I may have had a little plastic surgery recently, but I'm still the same person.' The reporter is not convinced, and nor is the crowd. 'Look,' says the actress, 'ask me anything you like about my career and I'll know the answer.'

Eventually the suspicious reporter is persuaded that she is indeed Maria Lorez. Although her appearance has completely changed, she still has all the *memories* of the famous film star.

Can you think back to your first day at school or your first ever holiday? Are you the only person who has those particular memories? Is it possible that the person sitting next to you could remember exactly the same experiences?

It seems unlikely that anyone else could have identical memories to you. And the fact that you can remember so much about your past is one way of knowing you're the same person you've always been.

So perhaps who you are depends on your memories.

... a bad memory

Then again, not everyone's memories are reliable. Illness, for example, can cause some people to forget even very recent experiences. Perhaps someone in your family has had a stroke. Or you may know someone who has Alzheimer's, a disease that has a direct effect on memory.

Just because someone loses their memory, they don't stop being themself. Even if someone becomes severely brain damaged (perhaps as the result of an accident), we don't consider them to be a completely new person. They may seem different to the way they used to be – we might even say that their *personality* has changed. But they aren't different in the way that you and your best friend are different. You and your best friend have two separate bodies. Someone with Alzheimer's, or someone who has suffered brain damage, has the same body they've always had. It seems that our bodies are important to who we are after all. But perhaps some parts of the body are more important than others.

Brain box

Diseases like Alzheimer's suggest a very strong connection between our minds and our brains. Of course, our brains are a part of the body. Just like hearts and lungs and kidneys, they are made up of *physical stuff* like cells, blood vessels, tissue, etc. But it's also natural to think of the brain as the place where our thoughts and feelings take place – almost as if it's the box, or container, of our mind.

Over the years scientists have discovered many other links between the brain and our minds. We know that blows to the head can cause memory loss or amnesia. And damage to the brain's frontal lobe can affect a person's ability to concentrate and solve problems. The frontal lobe is the bit of your brain directly behind your forehead, and believe it or not, removing part of it used to be a medical procedure. It was often used to treat mentally ill patients, particularly in the 1940s and '50s. This practice of lobotomising people finally began to die out in the 1960s as most doctors came to regard it as brutal and dangerous, even though it occasionally produced successful results.

An interesting story concerning the link between brain damage and personality involves a 19th-century Canadian railway worker called Phineas Gage. In 1848, an accidental explosion blasted a 3 metre long iron rod straight through his skull. Remarkably, Gage survived. Indeed, he didn't even lose consciousness. Following his appalling injury, however, he ceased to be the calm, thoughtful person he'd been before. Instead he became known for his aggressive temper and a tendency to swear at everyone he met. Not surprisingly, he became something of a curiosity and spent a year as the star attraction at a museum in New York. People would come from miles around to gawp at both him and the iron rod itself. But Gage also attracted the interest of the scientific community, who began to conduct detailed research into how brain damage affects who we are.

The brain-swap machine

Dr Ghaffari has always been convinced that it's our thoughts, feelings and memories that makes us who we really are. And knowing all about the connection between brains and minds, he designs an experiment to test his theory.

After months of preparation, the eminent scientist Dr Ghaffari has asked his assistant Dr Harrop to put on a strange metal helmet and stand in a specially constructed glass pod. These form part of the doctor's new brain-swap machine.

Dr Ghaffari explains that he will enter another pod and put on a second helmet connected to Dr Harrop's by two rubber tubes. He will then pull a lever to start the experiment.

Inside the helmets are sharp round saws designed to cut holes in people's heads. In a matter of seconds, Dr Ghaffari's brain will be sucked along one tube into Dr Harrop's head, while Dr Harrop's brain is sucked along the other into Dr Ghaffari's.

With the experiment complete, Dr Ghaffari believes he'll have demonstrated that who we are only depends on our brain. 'After all,' he declares, 'I will still be *me* once my brain is in your body, and you will still be *you*, even though your brain is in my body.'

With these words, he reaches for the 'on' switch ... only to discover that Dr Harrop has fled the building.

Monkey business

If you think this experiment is completely deranged, you may like to know that scientists have conducted similar real-life tests with animals. In 1970, an American Professor called Robert White attempted to transplant one monkey's head onto the body of another. The first monkey survived for a short time after the operation!

Imagine if Dr Ghaffari's experiment had been a success. Do you think he would have been the same person if he'd had Dr Harrop's arms and legs and stomach and chest? Will we always remain the same people as long as our brains remain intact?

★

Naturally, Dr Ghaffari is upset that he's been unable to conduct his experiment. But he can understand Dr Harrop's objections to having his head sliced open, so for his next experiment he decides to build a robot assistant. And this time he sets out to prove that who we are doesn't even depend on our brain.

The brain-copier

Dr Ghaffari is determined to make the most life-like robot he can. All its bits are made of a rubbery material, just like human tissue, and electrical impulses are zapped along thousands of wires, just like a human nervous system.

Dr Ghaffari also designs a new version of the brain-swapping machine. He calls it the brain-copier, and when activated, it will copy all the thoughts and memories in Dr Ghaffari's brain and beam them straight into a microchip in the robot's head.

If this experiment works, it will seem to show that who you are doesn't rely on your *physical* brain after all. It will support an idea we looked at earlier, that who we really are actually depends on the *non-physical* thoughts and feelings of our minds.

Having made his final conclusions, Dr Ghaffari is just about to flick the 'on' button when a puzzling thought crosses his mind.

'If the experiment works, who'll be the real me?'

What if?

Perhaps you are thinking, that's all very well, but Dr Ghaffari's experiment is actually impossible. It's true no real brain copiers has ever been invented, but philosophy is all about asking 'what if?' Thoughts and feelings can't be copied from one body to another at the moment, but let's imagine what would happen *if* they could. What if everything that's in the Doctor's mind could be successfully copied into the robot's head? What exactly is Dr Ghaffari worried about?

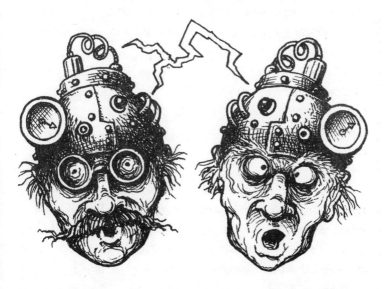

The problem is that, if the experiment were to work, there would be *two* people in the room with exactly the same thoughts and memories.

But think back to the very beginning of this chapter. We asked the question what makes you *you* and not somebody else? It just doesn't seem to make sense to say that you could be two people at the same time.

Perhaps the skin-and-bones doctor would be more real than the robot doctor. But if that's the case, it suggests that the physical body you're born with is important to who you really are after all.

As is often the case in philosophy, the question of who we really are takes us in very different directions. One the one hand, it seems that our bodies aren't very important. One day we might be able to replace every single bit of them. Then again, who we are can't depend only on our thoughts and feelings, because if those could be copied into several other bodies, we wouldn't be unique anymore. There could be any number of identical 'you's walking around! (In the *Science and Scientists* section we'll look more closely at the issue of **cloning**. As we'll see, this process involves the creation of plants or animals that are at least genetically identical.)

The man who doubted everything

So far, we've assumed that minds and bodies are made of very different kinds of 'stuff' – physical stuff, like bones, and non-physical stuff, like thoughts. This idea can be traced back to the 17th-century French thinker **René Descartes**.

Descartes' claim to fame was that he doubted almost everything. For one thing, he was worried that the outside world might actually be some kind of illusion. It was possible, he argued, that some evil demon (a sort of bad god) was tricking him into thinking the world existed, when actually it was just a figment of his imagination. For all he knew, this bad god might even be controlling his mind, making him believe that 2 + 2 was 4 when the real answer was 5. (As we saw in *Truth and Knowledge*, this is an example of a sceptical argument.)

But the most terrifying thought of all was that maybe he didn't even exist!

After many sleepless nights, Descartes discovered to his relief one thing he could be sure of. If he was being deceived, then there must be a 'him' that the deception was happening to. The fact that he was worrying about these problems at all meant that his mind, at least, had to exist. 'Cogito ergo sum' (I think, therefore I am), he declared – neatly coining philosophy's most famous sentence.

Descartes thought he'd proved that his mind *must* exist, even if his body didn't. And this made him think that minds and bodies must be very different sorts of things.

We've already noted that bodies can be seen and touched. They're made up of atoms and molecules and have physical properties like size, weight and shape. Minds, on the other hand, are made up of thoughts and feelings, which don't have any physical properties. You can point to a football but you can't point to a thought. You can't say that a particular feeling is green or six foot tall.

Minds versus bodies

The idea that we all have both a mind *and* a body is very natural. But the question of how the two interact raises some rather awkward problems, especially if they're different, as Descartes believed.

Let's consider bodies by themselves. Like all physical objects, they obey certain scientific rules, in particular, the rule of **cause and effect**.

In its simplest form, this rule says that every physical action has been *caused* by previous physical actions. For example, the movement of a football is caused by the movement of your foot. The movement of your foot is caused by the contraction of your muscles. Your muscles contract because they've received electrical signals from your brain and so on.

Even on a microscopic level, atoms and molecules move in the way they do because they've been hit by other atoms and molecules.

So here's the big puzzle:

> **Since the rule of cause and effect means every physical action can be explained by other physical actions, how can *non-physical* thoughts or feelings cause anything at all?**

And yet, as we've seen, feeling embarrassed really does seem to cause our cheeks to undergo a physical change. And stubbing our toe really does seem to cause a feeling of pain. How is such interaction possible between physical bodies and non-physical minds?

A disappearing act

Here's a possible, if rather surprising, answer to the question:

Descartes got it wrong! There aren't two different types of 'stuff' at all. Minds and bodies are made from exactly the same thing. And since there's only one type of stuff in the world, the problem of interaction simply vanishes.

What's the matter?

One version of this theory is known as **materialism** (the term comes from the word 'matter'). Materialists argue that the non-physical mind is just an illusion, and that our thoughts and feelings are nothing more than chemical reactions in our brains. The argument goes something like this:

Whenever you stub your toe, changes take place in your body. Electrical signals are zapped along your nervous system to your brain, where they trigger a series of chemical reactions. In everyday language, we might say these changes *cause* us to feel pain, as if pain itself is something extra, something more than the actual *physical* changes that occur. But Materialists believe it's a mistake to think of pain in this way. They argue instead that pain simply *is* the chemical and electrical reactions in question.

Here's another example:

For Materialists, the feeling of pleasure that comes from eating an apple isn't caused by a particular chemical process, it is *identical* to it. You can describe that process in technical language (involving complicated scientific equations) or you can refer to it as 'what it *feels* like to enjoy an apple'. But whatever you call it, the two things are the same, just in the way that H_2O is another way of describing water.

Talking about feelings is just a different way of describing the same physical process. So the problem of interaction between physical and non-physical 'stuff' disappears.

Can a robot think?

Many of today's scientists are involved in developing machines with **artificial intelligence** or **AI**, and for many years computers have been able to carry out tasks as well, if not better, than human beings. (Even a simple calculator is better at maths than most people.) But the greatest challenge will be to create a machine that can actually think for itself.

If Materialists are right, and human thoughts and feelings are nothing more than chemical reactions, scientists have a good chance of achieving their aim. They'd have to identify all the tiny particles that make up a human body, and understand all the possible reactions that take place within it. But as long as these could be copied into artificial brains and nervous systems, the robot's thoughts should take care of themselves.

Robot exams

In 1950, the scientist Alan Turing proposed a way of testing machines to see if they could actually think like people. Turing believed that we'd never be able to see the process of thought itself. However, we can see the results of thinking, in the form of speech or writing, for example.

In order to conduct his Turing Test, he imagined sitting in a room and typing out a series of questions. The questions would then be answered separately by the machine being tested and a human being. If Turing was unable to tell which answers had come from which source, he would have to assume that the computer had the same ability to think as the human being.

Alan Turing lived an extremely interesting, and ultimately tragic life. During the Second World War he worked for British Intelligence at Bletchley Park, trying to crack German military codes. In 1940, he played a major role in deciphering the Enigma machine, which was used by the Germans to encrypt top secret messages.

However, during the 1950s it was discovered that Turing was homosexual. Shockingly, this was against the law at the time and Turing was prosecuted for indecent acts. Rather than face imprisonment he agreed to medical treatment aimed at 'curing' him. This treatment proved so distressing that in 1954 he took his own life.

By the way, Bletchley Park is now a museum which is open to the public. If you're interested in spying and code-breaking, visit the website at http://www.bletchleypark.org.uk/.

Robot rights

If a robot could think for itself, we might have to give it certain rights, like the right not be attacked or destroyed. It wouldn't seem very fair to unscrew a robot's head if it experienced pain and sadness just like we do. (We'll look at the question of rights more closely in the *Right and Wrong* section.)

Can philosophers tell jokes?

Q: What thinks like a bat, feels like a bat and has the memories of a bat?

A: A bat.

If you heard that joke at a party, you probably wouldn't be very impressed. But even if it isn't very funny, it does illustrate a problem with the point of view we've been exploring.

You see, according to Materialists, thoughts and feelings are just chemical reactions. And chemical reactions can be written down in the form of scientific equations. Once you've done that, there's no reason why anyone couldn't look at and study them.

To put it another way, you wouldn't have to be a bat to know all about bat feelings. You'd just have to look at a series of scientific descriptions.

But some philosophers insist that our private experiences could never be seen by everyone in this way. For example, how could anyone really understand what you were experiencing if you sat on a drawing pin? It wouldn't matter at all that a scientist was able to explain all the chemical reactions going on in your brain. What you *feel* would only be known by *you*.

A bat experiences the world in a *particular* way. It responds to sounds in a particular way, hunts in a particular way and experiences pain in a particular way. Indeed, all its experiences are particular to it. A bat's experience belongs to the bat, and no one else. Even if we understood all the chemical reactions that go on in a bat brain we wouldn't know what it actually felt like to be one. That's something only the bat can know.

So maybe our thoughts and experiences can't be completely described by chemical reactions after all.

The question of what it might be like to be a bat was first posed by the American philosopher Thomas Nagel. He chose a particularly interesting example, because a bat's experience of the world is so different from our own. For instance, although they're not quite as blind as generally thought, they hardly use their sight at all to travel around. Instead, they use a system of echolocation. By sensing the time taken for the sounds they make to bounce off objects in their path, they can judge both distance and direction. If you've ever been in a tunnel and experienced your words echoing off the walls, you'll be able to grasp the basic principle.

Is life just a dream?

We've seen that Materialists believe there's no such thing as non-physical thoughts and feelings. They've tried to show that everything boils down to chemical reactions, but run into difficulties thanks to a colony of bats. (A colony is the word for a group of bats, by the way).

Let's finish this chapter by looking at a completely different approach, put forward by a group of philosophers called **Idealists** (we'll see why in a moment). Like the Materialists, Idealists believe there's only one type of 'stuff' in the world. Only for them, that stuff is non-physical. Physical bodies are just figments of our imagination!

So is this argument convincing?

Well, think for a moment about what happens in our sleep. Isn't it true that, when we dream, our minds invent whole worlds to explore? We bump into friends and strangers, visit familiar places as well as distant lands. And yet, as soon as we open our eyes, the dream-world disappears. All the physical things we thought were real were actually nothing more than illusions, or ideas in our mind.

Is it possible that what we think of as our waking life is also just a dream? How can we know that everything we see around us isn't just a product of our imagination? And of course, if there really is no physical universe, the question of how minds and bodies affect each other won't ever trouble us again.

Are you all alone?

One problem with this argument is that it can lead to something called **solipsism**. Solipsism claims that, since you can't *prove* your whole life isn't a dream, you can't be *certain* that anything exists outside your mind. Your home, your school, even your family may be nothing more than ideas in your head.

Solipsism is another example of a sceptical argument (we also ended *Truth and Knowledge* with one of these). Like many sceptical arguments, it's surprisingly difficult to show it's wrong. You might think it's obvious that other people and objects exist. But how can you actually prove it?

Right and Wrong

Philosophy isn't just about who we are and what we know. It's also about what we *do* and what makes our actions right or wrong. This is the branch of philosophy known as **ethics**, and whatever we do in our lives, important ethical questions are never far away.

For example, have you ever woken up in the morning and thought, 'I can't be bothered to go to school today. I'd rather stay at home and watch TV.'? Most people have probably had similar thoughts at one time or another. But why is it that, deep down, we know we'd be doing something wrong? One reason could be that staying in bed might involve lying to your family and pretending to be ill. People have a feeling that telling lies is the wrong thing to do.

If you wrote out all the other things you thought were wrong, your list might include the following:

- Robbing a bank
- Killing an animal
- Breaking a promise
- Committing murder
- Telling a lie
- Planting a bomb

Some of these, like murdering someone or robbing a bank, seem pretty obvious. Others are more controversial – in this chapter we'll look particularly closely at the issue of killing animals.

We'll also ask if people should be punished for doing the wrong thing, and see if there are any rules we can follow to help us keep on the right track. And then we'll consider governments and why we're expected to obey the laws they set down. We'll end the chapter with a look at terrorism, and see why now, more than ever, it's important to think through ethical questions for ourselves.

By the way, in this chapter we're going to be talking quite a lot about assumptions. Assumptions can be thought of as beliefs and opinions that we often take for granted. For example, we probably all *assume* that killing is wrong. But as we've seen throughout this book, philosophy is all about questioning what we think we know.

★

Questions of right and wrong are rarely black and white, and thinking about them requires a clear head. You might want to warm up your brain with the following intriguing problem:

The runaway train

Imagine you're walking beside a railway line when you see a train hurtling towards a fork in the track. The train looks like it will veer to the left and hit two children playing on the rails.

Fortunately, you spot a lever which will change the direction of the train. But if you re-route it down the right-hand fork, it will crash into a man walking his dog over the level crossing.

You only have seconds to make a decision. You could:

1. Ignore the lever. You didn't cause the situation, so you don't need to get involved.

2. Pull the lever, switching the direction of the train and killing the man and his dog.

What is the *right* thing to do?

By the way, this is what's known as an **ethical dilemma**, a situation in which you're asked to make a very difficult choice between two options.

Perhaps you chose the second answer. If so, what were your reasons? Maybe you thought it was more important to save two children than one man.

But now imagine the man was your grandfather. How would that affect your decision? Would you change your mind if there were ten men on the right-hand track rather than just one? What if those ten men were all criminals?

Thinking about 'The Runaway Train' is a good way of testing your response to ethical problems. By changing the details of the story, you can get a sense of the beliefs that are important to you. For example, did you think it was better to kill one man and his dog rather than two children? Perhaps that's because you believe human life is more important than the life of an animal?

And did you have less sympathy for the ten men once you thought they might be criminals? Do criminals have fewer rights than other people?

Luckily, you're unlikely to face a situation like this in your life. But that doesn't mean you won't have difficult choices to make. And in every case, your decisions will be influenced by other beliefs and assumptions. It's important to recognise what they might be, and whether you have good reasons for holding them.

So now your brain's suitably warm, let's plunge into one of philosophy's biggest ethical dilemmas – one that has a direct impact on our daily lives.

Animal rights: the big debate

Throughout history, people have assumed very different things about how animals should be treated. In Ancient Egypt, many were thought to have divine powers. (Harming a cat was even punishable by death.) Many Buddhists are vegetarians because of a pledge they make never to destroy life. And today, many Hindus continue to consider the cow sacred for the nutritious properties of its milk. In the West, however, attitudes have been strongly influenced by the Christian belief that God put animals on earth to fulfil human needs. The following is a direct quotation from the Bible (*Genesis*, book 1, verse 26):

> And God said, let us make man in our image, after our likeness: and let them have dominion* over the

*'Dominion', in this sense, really just means 'power'.

fish of the sea, and over the fowl of the air, and over the cattle, and over all the earth, and over every creeping thing that creepeth upon the earth.

Today, people continue to use animals for their own ends. Not only are countless numbers killed for food and clothes, but many are subjected to gruesome experiments in the interests of scientific research. Others are killed for sport, while many have also died in brutal human conflicts. In the First World War alone, 8 million horses, donkeys and mules were killed. In 2004, a memorial to animals lost in war was erected in London. You can visit it yourself on Park Lane near Hyde Park.

Where do you stand?

Perhaps you already have strong views on the right way to treat animals. But have you ever asked yourself what assumptions those views rely on?

For example, Paul sees nothing wrong in polishing off a plate of sausages, but like most people he wouldn't dream of eating another human being. Jenny thinks that makes him guilty of double standards. She thinks his belief is based on the assumption that people are different from other animals.

However, in 1859, the naturalist **Charles Darwin** turned this idea on its head. In his book *The Origin of Species*, he proved that all living things, including human beings, are a product of evolution. Scientists have now traced our ancestors back to great apes and beyond. In fact, all animal life probably began in the sea. Humans may be remarkable animals, but they're animals nonetheless. (We'll explore Darwin's ideas in much more depth in *God and Nature*.)

For Jenny, the issue of how similar we are to other animals is at the heart of the animal rights debate. She believes that, if it's right to eat some animals (like sheep or cows), it ought to be OK to eat all animals (including human beings). Or to put it another way, if it's wrong to eat humans, it should be wrong to eat other animals too.

That's all very well, thinks Paul, but surely Jenny's wrong to assume that every animal should be treated the same. Killing a human being is much worse than swatting a fly. You have to draw a line somewhere or we'd be in the wrong every time we accidentally trod on an ant.

But drawing the line between humans and other animals isn't as easy as you might think …

The animal tool kit

Scientists used to believe that our ability to make tools was one thing that separated us from other animals. Even cavemen deliberately constructed flint-tipped spears in order to kill woolly mammoths and built fires in order to cook their meat.

However, during the 1970s, studies of apes and monkeys showed that animals make and use tools in a very similar way. Chimpanzees use stones to open nuts and bundles of leaves to scrub their bodies. They also use sticks to remove termites from their nests, often chewing them with their teeth to mould them into shape. (Maybe this isn't surprising given that chimps share more than 99 per cent of our **DNA** – the chemical that makes up our **genes**.) However, in 2002 a small black crow called Betty shocked the scientific world. By bending a piece of wire with her beak, she made a hook with which she was able to extract food from a small container. Betty had never come across wire before and yet she seemed to know exactly what to do with it. Just like a human being, she spotted a problem and found a way to solve it. As Jenny explains to her brother, the fact that animals can design tools suggests they're much more like us than we once thought.

By the way, if you want to see Betty in action you can log on to: http://users.ox.ac.uk/~kgroup/trial7_web.mov.

Mathematical horses

Paul's heard all about Betty the crow, but he also knows a rather interesting story about a horse.

At the end of the 19th century, a Russian nobleman called Wilhelm Von-Osten argued that animals could be taught things in the same way as humans. To prove his point, he bought a horse called Hans, and with the help of an abacus and a blackboard he started to teach it simple mathematics.

Von-Osten's experiment was surprisingly successful and soon the horse was able to work out complex sums. He'd tap the answers out with his hoof and got a carrot for every correct answer. People came from all over the world to see Von-Osten's amazing horse, which soon became known as Clever Hans.

Eventually a sceptical scientist called Oskar Pfungst paid Clever Hans a visit and noticed a puzzling fact. It seemed that the horse could only give correct answers when those watching knew the answers themselves.

At last Pfungst guessed the horse's secret. He realised it couldn't actually do maths at all. Instead, he'd learned to sense tiny changes in the body-language of the spectators. Whenever a sum was put to Clever Hans, he would slowly begin tapping with his hoof. As he got closer to the right answer his audience would lean in to look more closely. Their muscles would tense with excitement and their breathing would quicken in anticipation. From the reaction of the audience when the answer was reached, Clever Hans would know to stop tapping, confident that a carrot would shortly be arriving.

In a way, Hans was as clever as his nickname suggested. Sadly, however, Von-Osten's experiment had proved a failure. He died bitter and disillusioned.

The story of Clever Hans shows the dangers of assuming other animals think just like us.

Can animals feel pain?

Even if animals don't think about the world in the same way as we do, there seem to be some experiences we do have in common, like the ability to feel pain.

Of course, we can't ask an animal if something hurts, but scientists have discovered that the chemicals released in our bodies when we're in pain are very similar to those present in wounded animals. Paul remembers when his cat fell out of the tree and broke her leg. He has to admit that she certainly looked like she was in pain then. Well, argues Jenny, if animals can feel pain, it must be wrong to harm or kill them deliberately.

Paul's still not convinced. Even if some animals do feel pain, it isn't necessarily wrong to kill them. After all, animals kill each other in the wild all the time. They do what they have to do to survive. No one thinks a polar bear is wrong for pouncing on a defenceless seal.

'Ah ha!' cries Jenny suddenly, 'That's the whole point! Animals might have to kill other animals to survive, but we don't. We have a choice, so we should choose not to do it.'

The idea of choice is extremely important to questions of right and wrong, as we'll see later in this chapter. And Jenny is right that, although meat is a valuable source of nutrients, we no longer depend on it for survival. Humans can live long and healthy lives eating only vegetable produce.

Animal experiments

This question of survival raises the complicated issue of animal testing. Animals, particularly mice, are often used in laboratories to test the effect of new drugs. Although the government lays down strict rules to prevent unnecessary suffering, countless animals have died to provide human beings with valuable medicines. For instance, the discovery of penicillin in 1928 by Alexander Fleming saved the lives of many people who would otherwise have died from diseases such as meningitis. Today, the use of penicillin in antibiotics continues to keep many fatal infections at bay. But before it could be given to humans, it was tested extensively on animals.

Do you think it's acceptable to test drugs on animals if it helps the survival of the human race? This idea seems to rest on the assumption that the protection of our own species is more important than the well-being of others. Many animal rights protestors believe it's wrong to inflict suffering on animals for our own ends.

To help decide how you feel about animal testing, try designing a **thought experiment** like 'The Runaway Train'. For example, do you think it would be acceptable for ten mice to die in order to save a single person? What about a hundred mice, or even a thousand? Would it make any difference if the person in question was a member of your own family? Where would you draw the line?

Human guinea pigs

Arguments in favour of animal testing rely on animals and humans having similar reactions to certain chemicals. But this can be a dangerous thing to assume.

In 2006, a group of men volunteered to test a new drug called TGN1412 at a hospital in London. The drug, made by a company called Parexel, was designed to treat diseases including leukaemia and multiple sclerosis. Within minutes of receiving the dose, four of the men suffered a severe reaction. At first they complained of burning sensations all over their skin as well as pounding headaches. In fact, the drugs had caused their internal organs to swell, and soon the volunteers were fighting for their lives.

Prior to the human trials, TGN1412 had been tested extensively on mice and monkeys. But despite our genetic similarities to other mammals, scientists can't know for sure how the human body will respond to new drugs. Although violent reactions are very rare, similar cases have led animal rights supporters to reject the argument that animal testing is the best way to develop human treatments.

The question of rights

One of the big issues in this debate is whether humans and animals should be treated in the same way. And this raises the central question of whether animals should have 'rights' in the way that humans do.

When we think of human rights, we tend to think of things such as the right to life or the right not to be tortured. Human rights are important because they state that all people should be treated according to the same principles, regardless of race, religion, wealth etc.

Sadly, throughout history, certain people have been treated as inferior to others, with terrible consequences. For instance, 2007 sees the 200th anniversary of the abolition of the slave trade. From the mid-15th century, Great Britain was involved in the practice of buying African slaves. The slaves were then transported to America and the West Indies, where they were sold for huge profits. Their treatment was so appalling that many never made it to these destinations, dying instead in desperately overcrowded ships on their way across the Atlantic. It's believed that many millions of Africans were traded in this way, but it wasn't until the beginning of the 19th century that the British government finally bowed to pressure to end the brutal practice.

There are also many examples of people living in countries where their own governments persecute them simply because of their race or religion. During the Second World War, 6 million Jewish people (many of them German) were slaughtered by Germany's Nazi government. And in Zimbabwe, President Mugabe has driven thousands of white farmers from their homes.

A belief in human rights can help to prevent such abuses in the future. Since they apply to everyone, if one government is seen to be ignoring them, other countries can try to act to protect those who are suffering.

Jenny believes that, if human beings have rights, other animals should too. After all, humans are just one species of the animal kingdom. Just because we're more powerful than other species doesn't mean we should abuse that power.

Who's responsible?

However, there is another important aspect to the question of rights. For human beings, they're often tied up with responsibilities. If someone breaks the laws laid down by society, certain rights can be taken away. (For example, sending someone to prison removes their right to freedom.) Although some people are convinced that a person's right to life should never be taken away, others argue that you should lose that right if you commit murder yourself. (This is why some people believe in the death penalty.)

The question of rights and responsibilities is a tricky one. It depends on whether you think rights are about a sort of agreement, or **contract**. Are there some rights that can't be taken away, or does having rights mean you have a responsibility to behave in a certain way?

Returning to animals, one thing seems certain: any

rights we give them can't be linked to responsibilities. A farmer can't sit down with a fox and say, 'I won't chase you with my gun anymore, but you've got to promise not to eat any more of my chickens.' If rights are about agreements, or contracts, animal rights can't quite be the same as human ones.

Making the right choice

As we saw earlier, the idea of choice is crucial to ethical questions. After all, we could only really punish someone for doing the wrong thing if they could have *chosen* not to do it.

But what if someone could show that human beings don't really have any choice at all? This idea isn't as crazy as it sounds. In fact, we've touched on it already in *Minds and Bodies*, where we explored the idea that every physical action has been caused by a previous one. The belief that everything happens because it's been caused by something else is known as **determinism**. And determinism doesn't leave much room for choice.

To help understand the idea, it's useful to imagine that events in the universe are like dominoes in a line. Each 'domino' falls when it's knocked over by the one before it. And from the moment the very first 'domino' falls, all the others are bound to fall too.

But if everything humans do is bound to happen in this way, it's hardly fair to punish someone for their actions. They couldn't have chosen to do things differently.

★

This possibility that human beings don't have any choice is disturbing, but it doesn't fit very well with our experience of the world. You may not be able to choose to feel better if you have a cold, but surely you could choose to stop reading this book if you wanted to. In fact, choice is so built into the way we live our lives, it's difficult to imagine what we'd do if we didn't believe in it.

Philosophers are still very puzzled by determinism, but let's accept for now that we can make certain choices for ourselves. Wouldn't it be helpful if we had some way of deciding whether those choices were right or wrong? A rule to help us do the right thing.

In the 19th century, a philosopher called **John Stuart Mill** put forward one suggestion. He believed that the right thing to do was always whatever would eventually bring the *greatest* happiness to the *most* people. For instance, he thought it would be wrong to steal because of the misery it brings to your victim. It also makes others afraid that their belongings will be stolen. Even if the thief gets pleasure from the things they've stolen, this will be outweighed by the suffering caused to everyone else.

According to Mill, the right actions are the ones that lead to the best results. However, this argument can lead to some surprising conclusions:

Guilty as charged

Judge Dean is famous for his ruthless sentencing, and when the notorious criminal 'Mongrel' McNeill comes before him for crimes against the animal kingdom, he happily orders life imprisonment. But as he's relaxing at home that night, an anonymous note is pushed through his letter box. It reads:

> The judge thinks for a moment. It's possible the wrong man's been convicted, but does it really matter? McNeill's a nasty piece of work and deserves to be locked up. Nobody need ever know about this note and, as he rots in prison, he'll remain a deterrent to other criminals. Releasing him now would make a mockery of the trial. McNeill might even become a hero, an inspiration to others.
>
> On balance, Judge Dean thinks it's much safer to keep him locked up. Even if he is innocent of this particular crime, it will be good for society to have him off the streets. The *right* thing to do in the circumstances is throw the anonymous note straight onto the fire.

If you were arrested for a crime you didn't commit, you'd probably hope you weren't up before Judge Dean. But hasn't he got a point in this case? In the long term, locking up McNeill could be doing society a favour.

Part of the trouble with Mill's idea is that it's very difficult to know what the long-term results of an action will be. Judge Dean may be convinced that locking up McNeill will lower the crime rate. But what if his prediction is wrong? The real criminal might go to the papers with another anonymous note. The judge's deviousness might be revealed and people could lose faith in the legal system, reducing its power and authority. Without an effective legal system, crime might flourish.

If this were to happen, we'd probably say that the judge was wrong to act as he did.

The idea that something's either right or wrong depending on how things turn out seems a bit fishy. Wouldn't it be more helpful to know if an action is ethical *before* we did it?

This was what the German philosopher **Immanuel Kant** believed. He wrote an enormously long book on the subject, which ended up with a surprisingly short conclusion – a rule for deciding if a particular decision would be the right one:

> *You should do something only if you would be happy for everyone to act in the same way.*

So, for example, we could check whether it would be wrong to burgle someone's house by considering what the world would be like if we all stole from each other. We wouldn't want to live in such a society because our own belongings would never be safe. Again, according to this test, it can't be right to murder someone just because you dislike them. If everyone did this, the world's population would quickly diminish and you might well get murdered yourself.

However, even this simple rule has problems, as Nathan and Jack are about to find out.

Mill and Kant may not have come up with the perfect guide to doing the right thing, but which of these approaches do you find most appealing? Do you think we need to know that something is right before we do it? Or is an action only right if it produces good results?

Is it ever OK to lie?

Nathan and Jack are walking along a country road when a strange man rushes up to them.

'You've got to help me,' he pants, 'I'm being chased by a psychopath. Promise me you won't tell him where I am.' Baffled, the two boys agree and the man promptly dives into a hedgerow.

Moments later another man appears brandishing an axe. He demands to know where the first man went.

'Into the hedgerow,' blurts Nathan. 'No no, back down the path,' insists Jack.

The maniac's eyes narrow and the axe quivers dangerously in his hand. He snarls at the boys and blunders on up the road.

'Why did you lie?' Nathan asks Jack, 'It's completely wrong. Where would we be if everybody lied?'

'Well at least I didn't break a promise,' says Jack. 'What would the world come to if everyone broke their promises?'

Nathan and Jack both seem to be using the same rule –

You should do something only if you would be happy for everyone to act in the same way.

Jack feels that breaking a promise is wrong and Nathan feels that telling a lie is wrong. Kant's rule doesn't seem to tell us what the right choice is after all.

Why have governments?

Whatever our own views about right and wrong, we're often forced to follow other people's rules – in particular those laid down by the government. But you might wonder why we should allow other people to make so many decisions on our behalf. Why shouldn't we be free to make up our own rules? Why are governments necessary at all?

One way of looking at this question is to imagine a world in which governments no longer existed and everyone was free to do what they wanted. Here's one example of what such a world might look like:

The state of nature

In a world with no government, there'd be nothing to stop you stealing whatever you wanted. Equally, there'd be nothing to stop the person you've stolen from chopping your head off in revenge. In this world, there'd be danger around every corner. Sleep would become a real problem, since you'd always have to be ready to defend yourself from attack. If you want to know what it would be like to live in a world without government or laws, watch a few David Attenborough nature programmes. Being completely free would be like being a tasty wildebeest, terrified of ending up as a hungry lion's lunch.

In August 2005, Hurricane Katrina caused terrible flooding in the American city of New Orleans. As the emergency services struggled to cope with the disaster, the normal rules of society seemed to break down. Shops were looted, and gun battles raged in the streets. It took several days before the police were able to control the violence.

According to many philosophers, this is exactly the kind of lawless behaviour that has made governments so necessary. Agreeing to abide by a strict set of rules is the best way to protect our individual interests.

How does the government actually work?

Over the centuries, many different systems of government have developed to ensure society follows certain rules. Two particular examples, which lie at opposite ends of the spectrum, are **dictatorship** and **democracy**.

A dictatorship is a form of government in which all power rests with a single person. Although it may be possible for a dictator to govern their country well, there have been many more examples of rulers abusing this power. Saddam Hussein is an example of a modern dictator. Under his regime in Iraq, many thousands of innocent people were killed, often for simply expressing different views or belonging to particular religious groups. Twentieth-century dictators such as Adolph Hitler and Joseph Stalin were also guilty of appalling acts of genocide (the deliberate slaughter of huge numbers of people from different cultural, religious or racial backgrounds). Under a dictatorship, a country's inhabitants have no real influence on their government's decisions.

One the other hand, a democracy is designed to allow people to have a say in the way the country is run. The United Kingdom is an example of a democracy.

In reality, UK citizens don't concern themselves with every decision that affects the country. Instead we vote for, or elect, a small group of people whom we trust to make choices for us. We expect the people we vote for to represent our interests, which is why our particular type of democracy is known as a representative democracy. Every four or five years a general election is held, which provides an opportunity for people to vote a government out, if they feel that it no longer stands for what's important to them. In the UK, there are three major political parties, the Labour Party, the Conservatives and the Liberal Democrats. All three claim they're the best people to represent the people's wishes.

In a democracy, everyone ought to have the right to vote, but in practice there are always restrictions. In the UK, the right to vote doesn't depend on your sex or the colour of your skin, but it does depend on your age. Nobody under the age of 18 is allowed to vote, nor anyone currently serving a prison sentence. There are also many people who can vote but forget, or choose not to.

Nevertheless, the principal behind democracy is that

everyone has their say. And if you happen to vote for the losing party, you just have to accept you were in the minority and put up with it.

In fact, in this country there's a big problem with that idea. The way elections actually work means it's possible for a party to become the government with less than 50 per cent of the vote. In other words, more people might have voted against the government than for it. This happens surprisingly often. In the general election of 2005, the Labour Party won even though only 35.3 per cent of voters supported them.

The reason for this is that people don't vote directly for the government. Instead they vote for what's known as their local candidate. That candidate will stand for election in a particular **constituency**, which is simply a particular geographical area. The candidate who wins in each constituency will gain a seat in the House of Commons, and become a Member of Parliament (MP). They will then be expected to represent the interests of all the people in their constituency (not just the ones that voted for them!). There are 646 constituencies in the UK, and the party with the most MPs forms the government.

In 2005, the Labour party won 356 seats and were able to remain in power for a second term. They had 55.1 per cent of all the available seats, but only 35.3 per cent of the votes. To help understand how this can happen, let's look at the actual results of three of the 646 constituencies:

Putney: total votes cast: 36,574

Party/description	No. of votes
Conservative	15,497
Labour	13,731
Liberal Democrat	5,965
Green	993
UK Independence Party	388

Lincoln: total votes cast: 36,857

Party/description	No. of votes
Labour	16,724
Conservative	12,110
Liberal Democrat	6,715
UK Independence Party	1,308

Inverclyde: total votes cast: 36,098

Party/description	No. of votes
Labour	18,318
Scottish National Party	7,059
Liberal Democrat	6,123
Conservative	3,692
Scottish Socialist Party	906

As we can see, the current system meant that Labour won two of these seats (Inverclyde and Lincoln) and the Conservatives won one (Putney). However, if we add up the total votes cast, we can see that, out of 109,529, Labour only actually won 50,539, or 46.1 per cent

Many people believe that the current system is unfair and support a different system of voting known as **proportional representation** (PR). This is a fairly complicated issue, and there's a lot of debate about different forms of PR. However, the basic idea is that the number of seats that each party has in the House of Commons should reflect the percentage of people that voted for them across the country, rather than the number of constituencies each party wins.

From this brief summary, we can see that a democratic government can't represent every single person's interests. But even if a particular government is supported by the majority of citizens, would the laws they set down necessarily be *right*?

★

As it turns out, there are plenty of historical examples where a government's actions were wrong, even though many people supported them. For example, it wasn't until the civil war in 1861 that slavery was finally abolished in the USA. (As we saw earlier, the slave trade had ended more than 50 years before.) Despite some opposition, the practice had long been supported by the American government. One of the biggest questions for ethics, therefore, is whether people have the right to stand up to a government, even if it has been voted for by the majority. And if so, should they do so by peaceful or violent means?

Peaceful protest

During the 1950s and '60s, many black Americans took to the streets in a campaign of civil disobedience. Almost a hundred years since the end of slavery, they still found themselves treated like second class citizens. Inspired by civil rights leader Martin Luther King, many were prepared to risk arrest and imprisonment for their beliefs.

King's campaign began in 1955, when a black woman named Rosa Parks refused to give up her bus seat to a white passenger. (At the time white people and black people would have been expected to sit at different ends of the vehicle.) Following Parks' arrest for this 'crime', King called for the company to be boycotted. For over a year the black residents of Montgomery, Alabama refused to travel by bus, causing huge financial problems for the public transport system.

The deadlock was finally broken on 13 November 1956, when the Supreme Court made racial segregation on buses illegal. During the campaign, King had himself been arrested and his house had been bombed. But despite continued opposition, he campaigned tirelessly and successfully for equal rights until his tragic murder in 1968.

Although King believed it was necessary to break laws in order to change them, he also believed passionately in peaceful protest. He insisted that black people should never use violent or destructive means to achieve their goals.

However, other individuals have rejected peaceful protest and resorted to more violent means to achieve their aims. Such people are sometimes referred to as 'terrorists', particularly by those governments or leaders whose power is under threat. Over the years, many people who have been labelled terrorists have claimed justification for their actions. You may be surprised to know that Nelson Mandela (the first black president of South Africa, 1994–1999) was once considered a terrorist.

South Africa has had a troubled history since the end of the Second World War. In 1948, an all-white National Government came to power and developed a policy of apartheid. This policy was designed to deny black people the same rights as whites. Mixed marriages were banned, and black people were forced to live in certain areas away from the white populations. The Bantu Education Act of 1953 even proposed that black children should go to school solely to learn the skills needed to work for white people. There were many opponents of apartheid, and often they were dealt with by shocking force. In 1960, police shot dead 69 demonstrators in the town of Sharpeville.

It was against this background that Nelson Mandela and the ANC (African National Congress) began to abandon their belief that change could happen through peaceful means alone. In 1964, he was charged with sabotage and attempting to overthrow the government. He remained in prison for 27 years while the brutal apartheid regime continued.

For Nelson Mandela, resistance by force seemed the only option in a country where the government itself was violent and corrupt. In the eyes of that government he was a terrorist, but the rest of the world viewed him as a hero. In 1993 he was even granted the Nobel Peace Prize.

On many occasions, Nelson Mandela referred to himself as a 'freedom fighter'. As we saw in *Arguments (and how to win them!)*, particular words and phrases can provoke very different responses from people. The word 'terrorist' conjures up extremely negative images of fear and violence. The phrase 'freedom fighter', on the other hand, is much more positive. It suggests that the person in question is striving for noble ends. Depending on which words and phrases you use to describe someone, it is possible to influence how others feel about them.

Terrorism today

Ever since 11 September 2001, the word 'terrorism' has had a very particular meaning. Approximately 3,000 people were killed in the aeroplane attacks in New York and Washington, and the hijackers were immediately denounced as terrorists.

In the aftermath of the tragedy, people across the world tried to understand the reasons for these terrible acts. What was particularly shocking was that the victims were innocent people going about their daily lives.

It's natural to believe that killing innocent people is wrong. It's even tempting to denounce people who do such things as evil, as the president of the United States, George W. Bush, has done. But if killing innocent people is always wrong, how can war, in which civilian casualties are inevitable, be justified?

In 2003, the USA and the United Kingdom, with other Western governments, invaded Iraq to topple Saddam Hussein. (One of the reasons was that they believed Iraq also posed a serious terrorist threat.) Many thousands of innocent Iraqis* have now been killed as a result of the fighting that has followed, many by British and American soldiers. So what's the difference between a terrorist and a soldier?

One answer might be that a terrorist is deliberately trying to cause pain and suffering. For a soldier, however, the killing of innocent people is a regrettable consequence of being at war. Some Western governments would also claim that, although the situation in Iraq is very bad, things would have been much worse if Saddam Hussein had remained in power. The war was necessary to make the world a better and safer place.

This argument takes us back to John Stuart Mill's ideas, which we looked at earlier. Perhaps the invasion should be considered 'right' as long as peace and security is eventually brought to the country.

However, a similar argument might also be made by the very people the West brands 'terrorists'. They could argue that they, too, are simply struggling for a better

*It's very difficult to know exactly how many people have lost their lives in this conflict. At the beginning of 2007, the United Nations estimated a figure of 35,000.

world, and that their violent actions are necessary to achieve it. Perhaps they would consider themselves freedom fighters, rather than terrorists.

Ever since the events of 9/11, the world has seemed a more frightening place. Governments have different ideas about how best to tackle terrorism, and military action in Afghanistan and Iraq has divided many people. The issues seem so complicated that it can be tempting to accept what politicians tell us, rather than trying to solve the problems for ourselves. But these problems won't be solved without clear thinking and fresh ideas. Now more than ever, it's important to form our own opinions about the world's troubles. It's necessary to try to understand the point of view of others, even if we believe they're in the wrong.

God and Nature

For many people, the biggest question of all is whether or not a God, or gods, exists.

That's because a belief in God can give a valuable sense of meaning to our lives. The idea that you could earn a place in an afterlife by obeying certain rules is also a comforting one. It means that our time on earth, however difficult and painful, has a purpose. Death is not the end.

But for other people, ideas of God and the afterlife are really just illusions – perhaps even dangerous ones. They argue that, over the centuries, terrible wars have been fought in the name of religious belief. And certainly today, conflicts between people holding different religious views, such as Jewish people in Israel and Muslims in Palestine, continue to make the headlines. Perhaps, if everyone believed that this life is all there is, we'd make more effort to preserve our lives and the lives of others.

On the other hand, religious difference is often only a part of the reason for countries, or people, being at war. Other factors such as poverty, scarce resources and struggles for land may be at least as important, if not more so. It can be easy to blame everything on religion, when many other issues are relevant too. There are also many examples of the benefits of shared religious beliefs. The Quakers, for instance, have a long and peaceful history. Formed in the 17th century, the religion has its origins in Christianity, although it now welcomes people from other faiths and backgrounds. The central belief is that some part of God exists in every human being and that every life is precious. Quakers live by guiding principles of respect, tolerance and non-violence, and actively work to improve the lives of those less fortunate than themselves.

There are hundreds of different religions and faiths. The three largest, Islam, Christianity and Judaism, all share a belief in one all-powerful, all seeing and all-loving God. Other religions, such as Hinduism, worship many different gods. And even people who have no particular religious beliefs may still have a spiritual dimension to their lives. But this chapter is not about particular religions, or whether one is better than another. Instead, it looks at the reasons why some people think a belief in God helps to make sense of the world, and why others have difficulties with that view.

We can start by looking at one of the most famous arguments of all for the existence of God:

A clever design

Pal and Zox are aliens from Min, an overcrowded planet several billion light years away. On behalf of the growing Min population, they're searching the universe for new places to inhabit. Flying past Earth one day, they decide to check it out.

Being the middle of winter, the beach they land on is deserted, but after a while Pal stumbles across a wristwatch half-buried in the sand. She's never seen anything like it and takes it to the spaceship to examine. With Zox's help she carefully inspects all the tiny cogs and levers, but neither of them can decide what the object is for.

Eventually they notice that the movement of the hands marks different stages of the day. 'I've got it,' shouts Pal. 'This is a machine to tell the time!' The machine works so well that Pal and Zox quickly draw another conclusion. Such an impressive object couldn't have been made by accident. It must have been put together by a brilliant inventor.

Thinking this proves that intelligent life already exists on Earth, the aliens take off in search of other planets.

In the 18th century, Bishop William Paley compared objects like clocks and watches to the even more elaborate creations found in nature. The human eye, for example, seems to be a masterpiece of design. Made up of thousands of microscopic parts, it allows the brain to form an image of the world around us.

If a watch must have been made by a watchmaker, thought Paley, isn't it likely that the world, with all its plants and animals and mountains and oceans, has also been made by a brilliant inventor? This was his argument for the existence of God – a God who was responsible for creating or designing such an intricate universe.

(You might remember that we looked at the right and wrong way to use comparisons in *Arguments (and how to win them!)*. How reasonable do you think Paley's example is?)

For many years this view, often known as **intelligent design**, was widely held and today many people still believe the universe is too amazing to have happened by chance. However, just 50 years after Paley's death, a new idea began to take off. Known as the **theory of evolution**, it offered an alternative explanation for the amazing complexity of the natural world.

Survival of the fittest

In 1859, Charles Darwin published a book called *The Origin of Species*, in which he argued that all living organisms are in a constant battle for survival. The plants and animals that do survive are those that are best able to cope with their environment. For example, a lizard with sandy-coloured scales will be able to hide from desert predators much more successfully than one with green and purple stripes. The animals that live longest will also reproduce the most, generating more offspring sharing their parents' characteristics (we'll see why in a moment).

But what if the environment suddenly changes?

During the industrial revolution in the 19th century, buildings in large cities became covered in soot. Dull, greyish-coloured moths, which had once stood out against clean walls and surfaces, were suddenly well camouflaged. Birds couldn't see them easily and picked off the brighter coloured species instead. As a result, the dull coloured moths were able to live longer and pass their characteristic grey on to their young.

Darwin called this process **natural selection**. But in fact, that's only half the evolution story.

Genius genes ...

Over the years, scientists have begun to understand more about the ways in which species change to suit their environment. In particular, they've discovered what actually happens when living things reproduce. It's during this process that copies of their **genes** are passed down to the next generation.

Genes are made up of a chemical called **DNA** and can be thought of as a kind of recipe book for your body. Sharp claws, blue eyes and rough scales, for example, are all caused by particular combinations of genes. This combination, sometimes known as a genetic code, is what gives living things their individual characteristics.

... and mutant moths

The process of reproduction, however, is far from perfect and mistakes in copying can lead to changes, or mutations, in the genetic code of some offspring. This is one of the surprising ways in which new varieties of species emerge. An example of how this works involves our grey-coloured moths. It was exactly these kinds of copying mistakes that led to their appearance in the first place. In fact, they were a mutant variety that would probably have died out if it hadn't been for the sudden change of environment. The grey moth may look like a clever bit of design; it's easy to believe God made moths grey just so they could merge with their surroundings. But actually, this ability came about quite by accident.

A prickly problem

A similar phenomenon has recently been observed in the hedgehog population.

Previously, hedgehogs' best form of defence from predators involved rolling up into tight spiky balls. Those that tried to run away were more likely to be caught and eaten – sadly hedgehogs are not fast runners. However, standing your ground doesn't have much effect against cars, which are now one of the greatest threats to hedgehog survival.

Those hedgehogs that happen to be better at running (thanks to their particular genetic code) stand a better chance against oncoming traffic. And as they live to breed another day, more offspring will be born with this ability to run. Rolling up in a ball may one day be a thing of the past.

God versus science

When the theory of evolution was first put forward, it was considered a very dangerous idea. For a start, it contradicted the Christian idea that God created the world fully formed in just six days. This idea originates from the Old Testament of the Bible and is often known as **creationism**. Religious leaders also pointed out that the Bible tells us the universe is only several thousand years old. This isn't long enough for a gradual process like evolution to have taken place. By the way, people who believe that religious texts, like the Bible, are *literally* true in this way are often referred to as **fundamentalists**.

The scientists' case was strengthened by the on-going discovery of fossils preserved in layers of rock or mud. The fact that simpler organisms were always found in older layers seemed to show how species were developing over time. Mind you, even fossils failed to persuade everyone. Some argued that they were merely evidence of God's early designs for the world. Almost like the sketches an artist makes before painting the final picture.

Even today, controversy surrounds Darwin's theory. In America, certain schools insist on teaching **intelligent design** in science lessons as an alternative to the theory of evolution.

★

Apart from intelligent design, however, there are other reasons to think a belief in God helps explain how the world began.

The first cause

Rehan doesn't follow any particular religion, but he still has a strong belief in God. His daughter, Jamelia, asks him to explain what this God is actually like.

'Whenever things happen,' begins Rehan, 'humans try to find the reasons why. Do you remember how your brother broke his leg?

'Yes,' says Jamelia. 'A tree fell on him in the garden.'

'And why did it fall?' asks her father.

'I suppose because it was a very windy day,' Jamelia replies. 'But before you ask, I don't know *why* it was so windy.'

'I don't know either,' says Rehan, 'but everything that happens in the world does have a cause, even if we don't know what it is yet. But what about the first thing that ever happened in the universe, the first link in the chain? Did that have a cause too?

Jamelia's puzzled. She agrees that everything must have a cause, but she doesn't think the chain can go back and back forever. The universe must have started somewhere. 'I suppose it can't,' she says. 'Not if it really is the very first thing.'

'Ah,' says her father, 'then that first link in the chain must be different from everything that follows from it. If it doesn't have a cause itself, it must be very special. *That* is what I believe God to be.'

Jamelia doesn't think her father can be quite right. If God caused the universe to begin, who caused God? Rehan's answer is that God's existence doesn't have a cause, but Jamelia finds that a hard idea to grasp.

You may have noticed that this idea of **cause and effect** crops up in other chapters, including *Minds and Bodies* and *Right and Wrong*. It's one of the central problems in philosophy.

Going with a bang

During the 20th century, scientists spent a great deal of time considering how the universe might have begun. A major breakthrough came in the 1920s, when the astronomer Edwin Hubble observed that galaxies in space were moving further and further away from each other. This seemed to suggest that the universe itself was expanding. (One way to understand this is to imagine a balloon with spots all over it. As the balloon is filled with air, the spots will move apart.) By thinking about this process in reverse, scientists began to argue that all the physical matter that makes up planets, stars, galaxies, etc. must once have been packed together in one single, incredibly dense, point. The Big Bang theory states that the universe started at the moment when this point suddenly exploded outwards. In the 1960s, the discovery of something known as 'cosmic microwave background' also indicated that our universe is cooling down. Working backwards again, this suggests that it was incredibly hot in the early stages of its existence.

But even the Big Bang theory doesn't solve Jamelia's dilemma. The question remains; what came before the Big Bang? Some scientists answer that by saying there was nothing before, time and space themselves began in the explosion!

Then again, perhaps it's possible the universe doesn't have a starting point. Maybe time *does* go back and back forever. Jamelia can imagine the future going on without ending. Perhaps the past goes back forever too.

Is God perfect?

In any case, Rehan's explanation hasn't helped Jamelia understand what God might be *like*. She'd imagined God to be extremely wise and powerful, not just a link in a chain, as her father believes.

That's what her friend Tom believes. For him, God is perfect in every way. 'Think of the strongest, cleverest, kindest person you can,' he tells Jamelia. 'That's God for you. Someone who can do anything they want – someone who's never second best.'

Jamelia can imagine that kind of a God, but doesn't see why they would have to exist.

Tom tries to explain. 'If God's the most perfect being you can think of, that being *must* exist. A God that's strong and clever and kind but doesn't actually exist is nowhere near as amazing as a God that's all those things *and exists as well*!

'But,' he continues, 'the God we're imagining is never

second best. God has to be real because otherwise we'd be able to imagine someone even better. And that's impossible!'

Jamelia has a feeling that Tom's argument's a bit too clever for its own good. After all, we could probably *imagine* the most amazingly perfect horse in the world. That doesn't mean it has to exist.

In fact, Tom's thinking is pretty similar to one of the most famous philosophical arguments of all time, the **ontological argument**. There have been many different versions of this argument. **Descartes**, who we met in *Minds and Bodies*, was a keen supporter. It's seriously tricky, so don't worry if you find it hard to make sense of. But if you're feeling really brave, it goes something like this:

Ontological argument:

Heath warning – this problem can seriously scramble your brain

Here is a **statement** that seems fairly reasonable:

A perfect God might not exist

But actually, says the ontological argument, this statement has to be false. How could a *perfect* God not exist? A God that didn't even exist could hardly be thought of as perfect!

But if the statement is wrong, and it's nonsense to say that a perfect God *might* not exist, surely we have to accept that a perfect God *does* exist!

How strong is God?

If the argument above turned your brain inside out, have a think about this, slightly simpler puzzle.

Tom believes God can do anything. Does that mean this all-powerful being could create a rock too heavy to lift?

The answer seems to be no. Surely God could lift a rock, however big and heavy it was. But then again, how can there be something an all-powerful God *can't* create?

How good is God?

One last thing is bothering Jamelia, and it's something many of us have probably thought about. If God's so great, how come so many terrible things happen in the world? How come the tree was allowed to fall on Jamelia's brother in the first place?

Tom suggests it was probably punishment for him being so annoying. Jamelia's tempted to agree, but often it seems that people suffer when they haven't done anything wrong. What about natural disasters like earthquakes and floods that kill thousands of people in some of the poorest parts of the world?

On 26th December 2004, a movement of the Earth's crust under the Indian Ocean caused a terrifying tsunami. A giant wall of water raced at hundreds of miles an hour towards the shores of India and Indonesia, claiming hundreds of thousands of lives. Tragedies like this can cause people to question their deepest beliefs. If God really is full of love and goodness, why are these shocking things allowed to happen?

The last word?

Tom agrees that it's hard to know why some things happen, but he trusts that God always has our best interests at heart.

This trust, or faith, is very important to Tom. He doesn't have all the answers to Jamelia's questions and knows he may never be able to prove to her that God exists. His faith is not something he can easily put his finger on, but it's a powerful feeling nonetheless.

How do you feel about this issue? Do you think you should only believe in a God if you can prove one exists? Or is proof unnecessary as long as you have faith?

The best bet

The 17th-century philosopher Pascal had a rather unusual solution to the question of God's existence. His thinking went like this:

If God exists but you haven't spent your life believing it, you won't get to heaven when you die. (In those days, most Christians thought non-believers were going straight to hell.) On the other hand, if you do believe in God, but when you die it turns out you were wrong, it won't make much difference. You won't get to heaven but nor will anyone else.

Pascal thought it was safer to be a believer *just in case* God exists. (You might feel that this idea, known as Pascal's wager, is a bit like having your cake and eating it!)

Art and Artists

Have you ever asked what the word 'art' means to you? Perhaps, when you think of a work of art, you imagine a beautiful painting – a landscape or a portrait of an important figure from the past. Or maybe you think of a piece of sculpture, a statue made of marble or bronze.

Then again, if you've seen any modern art you'll know that paintings and sculptures come in very different shapes and sizes. Jackson Pollock made his name splashing random squiggles of colour onto enormous canvasses. His paintings look like huge plates of Spaghetti Bolognese and yet he's regarded as one of America's finest artists. And in the 1990s, the British artist Damien Hirst caused a stir when he placed the pickled body of a shark into a huge glass container and called that a work of art. (This exhibit goes by the weird title, 'The Physical Impossibility of Death in the Mind of Someone Living'!)

At the time, many people were shocked by Damien Hirst's work, but throughout history artists have faced opposition to new ideas. The Impressionists were a group of painters who emerged in the late 19th century. They experimented with colour to help the viewer capture the *feeling* of looking at a landscape. At first this new movement was ridiculed, but now their paintings can sell for millions of pounds and appear on countless posters and postcards. (You may have seen some of Claude Monet's famous paintings of water lilies.) Then in 1917, just as the art world was getting used to Impressionism,

Marcel Duchamp claimed he'd created a masterpiece by attaching a porcelain toilet to a gallery wall!

Of course, the term 'art' doesn't just refer to painting and sculpture. Photographs and films can be works of art, as can the plays of Shakespeare, the poems of Wordsworth and the music of Mozart. We also use the word 'artist' to cover a wide range of professions – musician, writer, painter, sculptor, actor, and more besides.

In this chapter we'll consider what different works of art have in common and whether there can ever be a definition of art that everyone agrees on.

We'll also look at another thorny issue for the art world – the problem of fakes and forgeries. We'll ask the question: does it really matter *who* makes a work of art as long as people enjoy it?

Tricky definitions

Before we try to define something as slippery as art, let's have a look at why good definitions are hard to come by.

Consider a very simple object, like a hat. One definition might be 'an item of clothing, worn on your head to protect you from the weather'. This certainly covers sunhats, waterproof hats and woolly hats. But what about hats worn just for fashion, or crowns, or party hats? The definition turns out to be too narrow. It rules out plenty of things we want to call hats after all.

Perhaps hats should be defined more widely as 'anything you wear on your head'. But isn't this too general? That definition fits a lot of things we don't usually think of as hats – a headscarf, for example. Or the hood of a jacket. Or even hair spray.

Can you think of a better definition of a hat – one that applies to every single hat you can think of? Try to make sure your definition doesn't also apply to something that isn't a hat at all.

You may find this surprisingly difficult. As we're about to see, finding a good definition of art is even harder.

But how's this for starters?

Is David Beckham a masterpiece?

Sarah and Jamelia are going on a school trip to an art gallery in London. They're hoping to spot some genuine masterpieces, but when they arrive many of the exhibits don't seem like art at all. In one room there's just a pile of bricks. In another there's a video of David Beckham asleep.*

Sarah and Jamelia prefer David Beckham to the bricks, but they're still unimpressed. Anyone can point a video camera at someone for a few hours. You wouldn't have to be a brilliant artist.

The two girls are so confused that they ask one of the attendants if these weird objects really are works of art. 'Of course,' replies the attendant. 'They're in a gallery aren't they?'

---

*Both of these artworks actually exist. The David Beckham video is often on show at London's National Portrait Gallery (www.npg.org.uk), although it's sometimes taken on tour around the country. As you can probably imagine, it's a very popular exhibit!

Perhaps, like Sarah and Jamelia, you aren't too happy with this definition. Surely there's more to art than this? If not, absolutely anything could be a work of art as long as someone puts it in a gallery. And anyway, this argument doesn't explain *why* some things are chosen to be exhibited and others aren't. The curator of an exhibition (the person who decides what goes in it) won't want to show just anything. Surely they'll choose the things they already think of as artistic.

Where is art?

Jamelia believes something is a work of art if it produces strong feelings in those who experience it. Certainly some paintings, poems and pieces of music can give us sensations of intense pleasure. Others have the power to disturb and upset us. Even David Beckham and the pile of bricks provoked some kind of response, so maybe they're works of art after all.

But what is it about a work of art that actually causes those feelings? What gives the work its artistic qualities? Jamelia thinks it may be something to do with the way it's been put together.

In the case of a painting, this might mean the way the artist has used the paint, or the way they've positioned the people and objects in the picture. Maybe, for it to be a work of art, all those lines, colours and shapes must have been put together in an artistic way. (In the case of another art form, like music, we might talk about the order of notes, melodies and so on.)

'Hang on,' says Sarah, when Jamelia explains this idea. 'All paintings have lines, colours and shapes arranged in some way or other, but only a few are proper works of art. How would you know if the way it was put together was artistic or not?'

'That's the whole point,' replies Jamelia. 'If it's a work of art, it must have been put together in an artistic way.'

But Sarah thinks this definition just goes around in circles. Let's look at the argument in greater detail to see why:

> Jamelia has decided that something's a work of art if it's put together in 'an artistic way'. But how will Jamelia know what 'an artistic way' is unless she already has some definition of art. And she can't already have a definition of art, because this is just what she's trying to find.

(It might help here to think back to *Arguments* (and *how to win them!*) and **circular arguments**.)

Are tin-openers works of art?

Let's try a different approach. Here's a simple definition that maybe everyone can agree on.

All works of art have been made by human beings.

Some people might even argue with this **statement**. Couldn't a beautiful spider's web, or the patterns on a butterfly's wings, be considered works of art? Perhaps, but when people say things like this they're usually speaking metaphorically. In other words, what they really mean is 'this butterfly is beautiful, *like* a work of art.'

But even if we do accept this statement, it's probably too general to be really useful. Tin-openers are made by humans too, and we wouldn't think of them as art.

Does art have a point?

One difference between a tin-opener and a painting or a piece of music might be that the tin-opener is made for a definite purpose – opening tins. Paintings, sculptures and sonatas, on the other hand, don't seem to have similar functions or aims. It appears they're created to be enjoyed *for their own sake*. Maybe this idea can help us find our definition. Perhaps a work of art can be described as follows:

> Something made by a human being that has no practical purpose.

Then again, isn't the enjoyment that art gives a kind of purpose? Don't films and books deliberately set out to entertain us? Before the invention of photography, artists painted pictures for the purpose of recording people's appearances, or even for propaganda. Portraits of Henry VIII, for example, were designed to show his subjects (as well as foreign powers) what a strong and powerful ruler he was. And throughout history people have created paintings, novels, poems etc. with the aim of earning money. Couldn't these examples be considered works of art even if they were intended for a purpose beyond enjoyment for their own sake?

The definition seems too narrow. It excludes many things we would probably like to call works of art after all. It also includes some rather strange objects. Imagine if you deliberately built a broken tin-opener. Would that be a work of art? You couldn't say it had much of a purpose.

★

Jamelia's beginning to think she'll never find a suitable definition. Maybe works of art don't have something in common after all. This feeling grows when, the day after her gallery visit, she goes to her great-grandmother's 100th birthday party.

Family connections

The party is an amazing occasion and Jamelia meets relatives she didn't even know existed. She's intrigued by how different everybody looks and yet, every so often, she sees a great aunt or distant cousin who reminds her of much closer members of her family. She also notices that, although her mother looks very like her grandmother and her grandmother looks very like her great-grandmother, her mother and her great-grandmother couldn't look more different.

On her way home she wonders if works of art might be a bit like members of a family. A painting of the countryside and a shark in a glass box may seem to have little in common with each other, but perhaps there's a third work of art somewhere which resembles both in different ways. Even if there's no one thing that all works of art share, maybe they're all part of one extended family.

Jamelia's excited by her idea, although she's not the first person to have thought of it. In the early 20th century, the philosopher **Ludwig Wittgenstein** suggested something very similar. He also believed that different works of art could share a kind of similarity, or family resemblance, without having to have any one thing in common. In fact, Wittgenstein though it was impossible to come up with fixed definitions for any objects and ideas, even very simple things like hats.

We've explored several possible definitions in this chapter, and found difficulties with all of them. The idea that anything in a gallery must be a work of art seems too general. The suggestion that art shouldn't serve any practical purpose seems too narrow. And Jamelia's theory of artistic qualities just goes round in circles. It's no wonder Wittgenstein's idea is appealing, and yet some philosophers still feel there must be a definition out there somewhere. If there isn't, how will we ever know if something's a masterpiece or not?

By the way, one of Wittgenstein's most famous examples involved trying to find the definition of a 'game'. As we've seen, he believed that perfect definitions were impossible. But perhaps you can prove him wrong?

Do artists matter?

Let's turn our attention away from definitions to the important relationship between artists and their work.

It's fascinating to know who painted a particular picture, or who wrote a certain book. But should knowing who the artist is influence our thoughts about the work itself? And what happens if we discover something's not by the person we thought it was?

Is it a fake?

In 1937, the respected art critic Abraham Bredius claimed to have discovered an unknown work by the great Dutch painter Johannes Vermeer. Vermeer only produced a handful of paintings during his life, and Bredius declared that this particular one, 'Christ and his Disciples at Emmaus', was a priceless masterpiece.

Eight years later an almost unheard-of artist called Hans Van Meegeren was arrested for selling paintings to the German Nazi Party. In his defence he claimed that the pictures were worthless fakes – painted by himself. He also confessed to having painted Bredius' beloved Vermeer.

The revelation shocked the art world and critics began to reassess the painting. Now they knew it wasn't a Vermeer, it was no longer considered a masterpiece and its value plummeted!

These days, critics point out Van Meegeren's clumsy use of paint and the picture's poor composition. They claim it obviously couldn't be by Vermeer. But perhaps this wouldn't have been quite so obvious if the truth had never come to light. The critics in the 1940s were excited to discover such a rare painting, and perhaps this affected their judgement about how good it was. Or maybe it was only the discovery it was fake that changed people's minds about its value?

The big question is, does it really matter who painted the picture? Why should the story surrounding Van Meegeren have any relevance to the artistic value of the painting?

Artists in context

Many people agree that works of art should be judged on their own terms, and that whoever created them is irrelevant. Then again, all writers, painters, composers etc. are shaped by the events that happened in their lifetimes. Studying the environment in which they produced their works can help us understand what those works really mean. For instance, in the late 19th century, the playwright Henrik Ibsen wrote a number of plays that condemned the way in which women were treated by society. Knowing that Ibsen was writing at a time when women weren't even allowed to vote helps us realise how shocking his plays were when first performed. Appreciating this context can give us a richer experience when we watch for ourselves, even if it doesn't affect the artistic quality of the plays.

Recreating the past

Some people go even further and suggest that the best way to appreciate art is to experience it as it was originally intended. So, the best way to enjoy a piece of classical music would be to hear it played on the instruments available at the time. (In Mozart's day there were no modern-style grand pianos.) And maybe Shakespeare's plays are best enjoyed in the sort of theatres that Shakespeare himself would have worked in.

One way of doing that might be to visit The Globe in London, a replica of the theatre where many of Shakespeare's plays were first produced (www.shakespeares-globe.org). Today, audiences can watch actors in period costumes on a stage similar to the one on which the first Shakespearian performers would have stood. When you're at The Globe it's easy to feel that you're stepping back in time. But it's also easy to forget the differences between theatre-going now and in the past.

Today, a trip to the theatre is often a special occasion, not least because it can be expensive. But 400 years ago, visiting The Globe was an everyday part of many Londoners' lives. The original building could hold 3,000 people, including noble men and women as well as commoners (who could buy standing tickets for a penny). With such a large number of people in one place, The Globe was also a breeding ground for disease. If you went to the theatre in 1600, there was a distinct possibility of catching the plague.

Theatres were also a place where political activists met to discuss plots against the King or Queen. To counter this, the government often recruited actors as secret agents. The famous playwright (and contemporary of Shakespeare) Christopher Marlowe was almost

certainly a government spy – a fact that may have con-
tributed to his murder in 1593.

Although we can learn all sorts of things from
The Globe, we can probably never fully recreate the
experience of seeing a Shakespeare play in its original
form.

★

Information about an artist's life can be fascinating.
That's why so many of us read biographies or watch
interviews with our favourite singers, painters, actors
and so on. But sometimes this information can have a
surprising effect on the way we view their work.

Bad influences

Sitting in the back of the car coming back from her great-grandmother's, Jamelia listens to a new album on her iPod. It's by her favourite boy-band and she thinks the music and lyrics are the best they've ever written.

That night, however, she happens to catch an interview with the band on TV. To her surprise, the singers turn out to be nasty pieces of work. They make all sorts of offensive remarks and even admit they think their own album's pretty bad.

The next day, Jamelia tries to listen again. But this time she doesn't enjoy the songs at all. Now she knows what the band are really like, she can't help looking for faults in the music. And when she thinks about it, some of the lyrics do seem quite clichéd. Disappointed, she decides to remove it from her playlist.

Jamelia's dilemma is similar to the one faced by the critics of Van Meegeren. It can be very difficult to separate our opinions about works of art from all the other things we know about the artist. Perhaps it would be better if we never actually knew who the artist was. Then we could concentrate on the qualities of the work itself.

Completing the circle

This suggestion takes us back to Jamelia's idea of 'artistic qualities' – things that works of art possess within themselves, something to do with the way they are composed, or put together.

We saw in the first part of this chapter how hard it is to define these artistic qualities. And there's another tricky problem. Our opinions about works of art often change with the passage of time.

During his lifetime, the Dutch painter Vincent van Gogh only managed to sell one of his paintings. Following his death, however, his reputation began to grow and sales of his work can now fetch millions of pounds. (You may have come across his famous paintings of sunflowers, painted in brilliant oranges and yellows.) Other artists, whose work was once thought extraordinary, are now largely forgotten. The musician Giacomo Meyerbeer lived at the same time as Mozart and was considered one of the finest composers of his time. These days his work has fallen out of favour and is rarely performed.

If works of art really do have artistic qualities, why is it that some people can see them, while other people can't?

Science and Scientists

Throughout this book, we've seen that philosophy is very good at asking questions, even if it doesn't always have the answers. Instead, it encourages us to think about problems in new ways and not just accept what we're told.

Science, however, seems to answer all sorts of important questions about the world. Science can explain why our feet stay on the ground (thanks to the law of gravity). It can help us get better when we're ill (thanks to discoveries in medicine). It can explain how different species adapt to their environment (as we saw in *God and Nature*). Scientists have shown us how to fly and how to send someone to the moon. They've allowed us to communicate using the internet and mobile phones. They've explained why metal expands when it's heated and why light can't travel round corners. They've shown why sweets make our teeth decay, and why water keeps us alive.

There are many branches of science, and they all address different questions. Physics examines the building blocks of the universe (atoms and molecules, forces and waves), biology explores living things and chemistry looks at the way substances react with each other. And within these branches there are many more specialised areas. There are microbiologists, particle physicists and biochemists.

These many branches of science don't just explain what's already happened in the world. By carrying out experiments and explaining the results, scientists can predict what will happen in the future. It's largely thanks to the experiments of environmental scientists that people are aware of the threat posed by global warming. And to find a way to prevent the dangerous rise in sea levels that results from melting ice caps, the world will certainly look to scientists again.

It's no wonder that people trust what scientists say, and believe that maybe one day they'll have answers to all our questions. But how exactly does science work? How do scientists make sure their experiments are accurate, and are their predictions as reliable as they seem?

In this chapter we'll look closely at the **scientific method** as well as considering some of the more controversial uses to which scientific knowledge can be put. In particular, we'll examine the issue of **cloning**, and consider whether we should ever put limits on what science can do?

Why trust science?

When Paul pops into the chemist for some painkillers, there are too many brands to choose from. One promises to be 'best-value ever!' Another claims to be 'new and improved!' Yet another has a picture of a smiling celebrity on the front. But one brand really catches Paul's eye. On the box is written 'scientifically proven to reduce all headaches'. Well, thinks Paul, if it's *scientifically* proven, it must be the best.

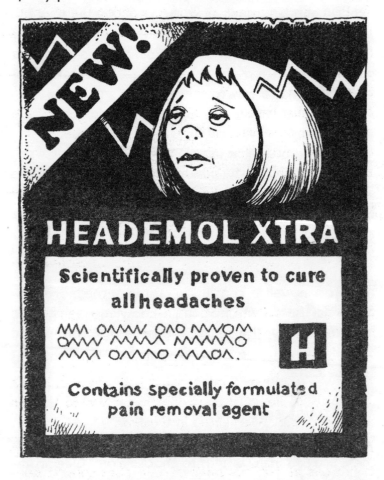

When Paul gets home he decides to go to bed with a hot drink. As he plugs in his kettle he considers how much he has to thank science for. For one thing, scientists discovered that water always boils at 100°C. And thanks to science, kettles can be designed to heat water to just that temperature.

As Paul sips his drink, he wonders about the scientific method. In the case of water's boiling-point, he imagines it works something like this.

Step 1 First, a scientist must have noticed, or observed, that heating water causes it to bubble.

Step 2 The scientist would have carried out more experiments to check that water always bubbles at the same temperature.

Step 3 The scientist would then have suggested an explanation for why the water starts to bubble.

Step 4 This would have formed the basis of a scientific theory – an explanation of what happened and why, which could be used to predict what would happen *whenever* water was heated in this way.

(Paul's example is actually slightly too simple. Water only boils at 100°C under certain atmospheric conditions, and it needs to be absolutely pure too, with no extra ingredients. If you heated water on top of Mount Everest, the boiling-point would be nearer 72°C because the atmospheric pressure is much lower.)

Seeing what you want to see

If Paul's view of science is right, the first step is crucial. If scientists make mistakes in their observations, their theories will be built on shaky ground.

This is also why we expect scientists to record what they see in an objective way. This idea of **objectivity** is extremely important in science. It means that a scientist must note down *only* what they see. They mustn't be influenced by what they expect to see, or by any beliefs they already hold. All they should be interested in is what's there in front of them.

But what happens when two people look at the same thing and see it very differently? Remember the rabbit/duck optical illusion from *Arguments (and how to win them!)*? Two people looking at that picture might see completely different animals.

When Paul was younger he went to hospital with a broken leg. When he saw the X-ray he could only make out a collection of vague black-and-white blotches. His doctor, however, was able to see exactly where the break was, and how it could be repaired. Paul and the doctor were looking at the same image, but the doctor's previous experience allowed her to see it in a very different light. Is it possible this could happen in science?

During the 17th century, arguments raged about whether the sun revolved around the earth or the other way round. If the astronomers Tycho Brahe and Johannes Kepler had witnessed the same sunrise, they would certainly have explained what they saw in differ-

ent ways. That's because Brahe clung to the mistaken belief that the Earth was a fixed point in the solar system. Kepler, however, was convinced the Earth moved around the sun. Again, this might remind you of the rabbit/duck picture, although there's at least a right answer here.

It's hard for scientists not to be influenced by their own beliefs. Even if they note down only what they see, they may not be quite as objective as they think. Scientists are just human beings, after all.

Predicting a problem

As we've seen, one of science's strengths is that it helps us predict what will happen in the future. Once we know that water has always boiled at a certain temperature, we know what will happen whenever we turn the kettle on.

Then again, how do we know that water has always boiled at that temperature? Surely no scientist has tested every drop.

Scientists can't repeat experiments forever. There must come a point when they think they've tested their observations enough to support their theories. In other words, having performed a certain number of individual experiments, they believe they have good reasons to make a **statement** like: water *always* boils at 100°C (as long as you're not up a mountain).

This kind of statement is sometimes referred to as a general rule. That's because it will *always* be true. Here are two other general rules of science: 'Metals always expand when heated'; 'All physical objects exert gravitational forces on each other'.

Often these rules come to be known as scientific laws, or even laws of nature. That's because they explain something definite about the way the world works. According to science, these rules (or laws) have always been true in the past, and must always be true in the future. (You might remember discussing statements like this in *Truth and Knowledge*.)

But here's a tricky question. How many experiments are needed before a general rule can be proposed? Ten? A hundred? A thousand? Surely, even if you've carried out a million experiments and got the same result, it's just possible that, the next time you do it, you'll discover something different?

Remember Dr Islan and Dr McDonald's quest for the Loch Ness Monster in *Truth and Knowledge*? Each time they tried to find Nessie, they were disappointed. Yet there remains the tiniest possibility that the creature does exist.

Even if water has always boiled at 100°C (given certain atmospheric conditions), isn't it at least *possible* that one day it will boil at a completely different temperature?

A bird's eye view

The 20th-century philosopher **Bertrand Russell** was very sensitive to the plight of turkeys. He suspected they were unaware of the possibility that the future might be different to the past.

Every morning on the turkey farm, at exactly the same time, the birds are given a delicious grain breakfast. As the days and months pass, they begin to believe, quite reasonably, that their 9 o'clock feed is as natural as the sunrise. So they get a terrible shock at 9 o'clock on Christmas morning when they're beheaded, basted and popped in an oven.

Perhaps this example is rather extreme. Being 99.9 per cent per cent sure of something isn't bad. Since water has always boiled at 100°C in the past, you might think it's at least *likely* to do so in the future.

But some philosophers are convinced there's no reason at all to expect the future to be like the past. Perhaps the most famous thinker to hold this sceptical view was **David Hume**, who lived during the 18th century. He didn't think we should rely on tomorrow being anything like today. A few hundred years later, someone else has a similar feeling …

Can you prove that the sun will rise?

On the first day of her new job, Anna bounds into the office with such excitement that her boss, Suki, thinks she must be nervous. 'No,' says Anna, 'just happy. The sun rose today. Isn't that great?'

Suki's glad that the sun rose, but doesn't think it's a reason to celebrate. The sun rises every morning and shortly afterwards she has to get out of her nice warm bed and come to work.

'You can't take these things for granted,' continues Anna. 'There was no reason to think it would rise today, and none to think it will tomorrow.'

'Nonsense!' snaps Suki. 'Even if there's a tiny chance the sun won't rise tomorrow, it's much more likely that it will.'

'No,' chirps Anna, 'you only think that because you think the laws of nature are the same every day.'

'But …' protests Suki, 'the laws of nature *are* the same every day!'

'Prove it,' says Anna, with a mischievous grin.

'Well, they were the same yesterday, and the day before that, and the day before that!' says Suki, losing her patience.

'Oh sure,' replies Anna, '*up till now* the laws of nature have always been the same. But how can we sure we'll be in the same boat tomorrow?'

'Because,' fumes Suki, 'the laws of nature are the same EVERY DAY!'

'Oh you can't use that old argument,' says Anna, triumphantly. 'That's just what I asked you to prove in the first place. That's like you saying "this apple is green" and when I ask you to prove it, replying "because this apple is green". I'm afraid you're just going round in circles.'

At which point Suki walks straight out of the room.

This is one of a number of **circular arguments** we've come across in this book. To refresh your memory, have a look back at *Art and Artists* and *Arguments (and how to win them!)*.

Even if Anna has a point, there's not much we can do about it, and most of us do expect the sun to rise. Nevertheless, this example, as well as the case of the Christmas turkeys, might make us begin to question whether scientific theories are quite as certain as we first thought.

Proving things wrong

We've seen that scientists have a hard job trying to show that what they say is 100 per cent reliable. There's always the possibility, however tiny, that a new fact will turn up and upset even the best theories.

In the middle of the 20th century, however, a philosopher named Karl Popper suggested it was more important for scientists to try to prove their theories wrong than right. Luckily, this is a good deal simpler.

Trying to *prove* that a statement like 'all cows eat grass' is absolutely 100 per cent certain is a hopeless task. Even if all the cows you've ever observed do eat grass, one might still exist somewhere that doesn't. On the other hand, it's perfectly possible to prove the statement wrong. All we'd need to do is find a single cow that won't touch the stuff.

That said, until we find such a cow, we should accept that 'all cows eat grass' is the best theory we've got. Indeed, it's very *likely* to be the truth. But if one day a cow turned up that only ate mud, scientists would have to replace their theory with a better one. In this way, thought Popper, science would always being moving in the direction of the truth, even if it never quite gets there.

Popper's idea has another useful function. It can help to show why some ways of explaining the world are scientific, while others are not.

What's your star sign?

As Paul lies in bed with his hot cup of tea and amazing headache-reducing pills, he glances at his horoscope in the paper.

Aquarius
You've had some highs and lows over the last few days due to the planet Mercury being upside down. But think positive and next week will bring some pleasant surprises.

Horoscopes, rather like science, try to explain why things happen in our lives and give advice on what to do next. But often they're so vague it's difficult to see how they could be wrong. If Paul does think positively and has a good week, it will seem the horoscope got it right. But even if he has a terrible week, it won't prove the advice was wrong. Perhaps Paul just wasn't thinking positively enough.

According to Popper, the great thing about scientific statements is that they *can* be proved wrong. That's what allows for new and better theories to take their place. That's how scientific knowledge makes progress.

For Popper, the mark of a truly scientific statement was that it could be tested. He believed that if a statement couldn't be clearly shown to be *either* true or false, it wasn't scientific at all.

You may remember that in *God and Nature* we mentioned an idea called **creationism** – the belief that the universe had been made by God in six days. This idea has sometimes been put forward as an alternative to **Darwin's theory of evolution**. However, it's exactly the sort of idea Popper would have rejected as unscientific.

That's partly because creationists are very unwilling to be proved wrong. As we saw in *God and Nature*, the discovery of fossils appeared to contradict the biblical account of how the world was formed. The creationist response was to claim that fossils were just a part of God's blueprint for the universe. This hadn't been a part of their original explanation, but they had to introduce it to protect their beliefs. It was as if they were determined to defend their original theory at all costs.

On the other hand, the theory of evolution could very easily be disproved. If we suddenly discovered human remains from 4 million years ago, it would be turned on its head. (Human's earliest ancestor, *Homo erectus*, is thought to have appeared between 1 and 2 million years ago.) However, such a discovery might help us devise a better theory, and scientific knowledge could continue to make progress.

Throwing the baby out with the bathwater

Popper's ideas can help us decide what counts as scientific knowledge. But how can we be sure that a theory really has failed a test? Even scientists sometimes make mistakes. Isn't it unfair to throw out an entire theory just because one piece of the jigsaw puzzle doesn't fit?

In the 16th century, Nicholas Copernicus was one of the first people to argue that the Earth revolved around the sun. This theory contradicted the widely held view that the Earth was the centre of the universe. However, scientists at the time were able to point out apparent problems with Copernicus' theory. In particular, they observed that planets did not orbit the sun in quite the circular motion he described.

Years later, improvements were made to Copernicus' system and further experiments proved his central idea to be right, even though it had contained some errors. It was lucky his idea hadn't been completely abandoned just because some of the evidence available at the time contradicted it.

Science, good and bad

Paul's headache pills are finally kicking in. The pain subsides and he starts to feel drowsy. He puts down his half-finished cup of tea and turns off the light. In the morning he'll wake up rested and refreshed. Medical discoveries are just one of the areas in which science has changed our world for the better. Next time you worry about going to the dentist, imagine what it was like for people before scientists discovered how to treat cavities and make anaesthetic. Toothache used to be one of the most painful afflictions you could suffer from, and ancient cures, such as washing your mouth out with urine, or eating mice, were very rarely effective!

But it's also true that, across the world, there are many whose lives remain untouched by the advances of science – people who have easily curable diseases, but can't afford the treatment they need. Or people who have no fresh drinking water because they lack purification tablets.

There are also those who've experienced some of the terrible uses to which scientific knowledge has been put. In 1945, the world's first atomic bomb killed 200,000 innocent people in Hiroshima in Japan. More recently, in 1988, Saddam Hussein used poisoned gas against the Kurdish population in Iraq. And every day, throughout the world's trouble spots, people are killed and maimed by bullets and bombs.

And then there are the environmental issues. Global warming now poses a serious threat to humankind and there's increasing evidence that we only have ourselves to blame. Although changes to the climate also happen naturally, the process appears to have speeded up thanks to the huge amounts of carbon dioxide we pump into the air. Much of this comes from burning fuel (like coal and gas) to generate electricity. In fact, carbon dioxide is only one of a number of greenhouse gases that contribute to this effect. Water vapour and methane are other examples. As these gases build up in the atmosphere, they trap the sun's heat as it's reflected back off the surface of the earth. As a result, the temperature of the planet rises.

Across the world, people have been slow to acknowledge global warming, and even today the reasons behind it aren't fully understood. However, most scientists now accept that the earth is warming faster than at any point in its recent history. If it continues to do this at its current rate, the consequences will be severe. One of the greatest problems is the melting polar ice caps. This is causing sea levels to rise and, within just a few decades, coastal areas around the world (including the UK) will be in danger of flooding. One way to combat global warming is to reduce the amount of energy we consume. Some ways of achieving this would include turning off the lights when we go out and not leaving our electrical appliances, like TVs and computers, on standby when we're not using them.

★

Even if scientific discoveries have occasionally done more harm than good, many people are still hungry for the knowledge that science provides. Throughout history, however, stories have been told about the dangers of knowing too much. Perhaps the most famous example, written almost 200 years ago, warned of the dangers of scientists 'playing God'.

Frankenstein

In Mary Shelley's famous novel (written in 1818) the young Dr Frankenstein sets out to discover the secret of life itself. Working alone in his laboratory, he builds a terrifying monster out of body parts from the local graveyard. Then, with the use of electricity (a new discovery at the time Shelley was writing), he brings the creature to life.

Tragically, Frankenstein's triumph turns to despair as he realises he can't control his creation. The monster causes havoc across the country until the doctor agrees to build him a companion. However, he's unable to complete the task and, in a terrible act of revenge, the monster murders Frankenstein's wife.

Frankenstein finally pursues the creature to the North Pole, where the harsh conditions prove too much for him. He dies in the company of a ship's captain to whom he has told his terrible story.

Today, Frankenstein's monster remains a powerful metaphor for the risks involved in meddling with nature. In particular, it's used by those opposed to advances in **genetic engineering** – scientific processes that deliberately alter the genetic code of cells to produce new characteristics. (You might want to have a look back at *God and Nature* to refresh yourself about these terms.) One of the most controversial forms of genetic engineering today is the practice of cloning.

Woolly thinking

In 1997, a research institute in Scotland proudly announced the birth of the first cloned mammal, a sheep called Dolly. This announcement divided opinion in the scientific community and beyond. Was it a major breakthrough with positive implications for science and medicine, or a dangerous attempt to interfere with nature?

A clone is an exact copy of something else. In scientific terms, an animal is a clone if its genetic code is identical to another's. In fact, identical twins are clones of one another. That's because twins form when a fertilised egg, or embryo, splits in two. Both these newly divided embryos share the same genetic code.

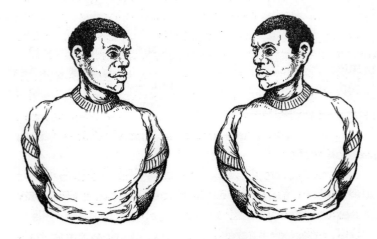

Some organisms are able to produce offspring by themselves in a process known as **asexual reproduction**. These offspring will have the same genetic code as their parent. (Bacteria reproduce in this way, as can certain plants and even animals like worms.)

In **sexual reproduction**, however, the male and female of the species both contribute equally to the genetic code of their young. In the natural world, all mammals reproduce sexually, which is why cloning a sheep was so remarkable. Dolly was created from a single adult cell, without the need for sexual reproduction. This is one reason why some people are uncomfortable with cloning. Human beings can now alter the ways in which life itself begins. The shadow of Frankenstein's monster looms.

But in fact, interfering with nature is nothing new. Building dams changes the natural flow of rivers and using fertilizers on crops artificially encourages growth. And for centuries people have used selective breeding in farming. In the case of cattle, for example, this might involve identifying the cows that produce the most milk and only allowing them to breed. The hope is that these cows will pass their desirable characteristics on to the next generation. In this way, farmers can influence the processes of **natural selection** that we looked at in *God and Nature*.

Human beings have always tried to control their environment. What difference does it make if they now do it on a genetic level?

One difficulty for supporters of cloning is the confusion over why it might be useful, or necessary. One hope is that it might one day be a solution for infertility. Parents who can't have children through sexual reproduction might be able to use cloning as an alternative. However, the possibility of cloning a whole human being (known as **reproductive cloning**) is a long way off – not least in this country, where such procedures are banned. A more realistic aim is the development of **therapeutic cloning**, which could be crucial in finding new cures for disease. One form of therapeutic cloning involves the artificial creation of embryos in order to grow particular cells. The complicated process works like this:

In the first stage an unfertilised egg is extracted from an adult female. In the egg, there will be a nucleus that contains half the genetic code needed to create a new life. (In sexual reproduction, the other half would be provided by the male sperm.) This nucleus is now removed from the egg, and replaced with one from another cell in the female's body. Since this new nucleus comes from an adult, it already contains both halves of the genetic code.

If the egg was now implanted back into the female, she could eventually give birth to a cloned offspring sharing her identical genetic code. (In simple terms, this is the process that produced Dolly the sheep). However, in therapeutic cloning, the growth of the fertilised egg is only allowed to continue for a few days. After that point, stem cells are extracted from it and the embryo itself is destroyed. These stem cells are of particular importance because they have the ability to develop into any cell in the body (in a process known as specialisation). It's this ability that raises so many exciting possibilities for medical science. It means that it might be possible to grow new cells to replace a person's damaged heart, lungs or even brain.

It's important to note that stem cells can also be extracted from embryos created from sexual reproduction, although in much smaller numbers than cloning allows for.

In 2002, human stem cell research was made legal in

the United Kingdom. However, the process continues to cause controversy. In particular, many people object to the destruction of the embryos, which is an inevitable consequence of removing the cells. Even if they have been artificially created, they have the potential to develop into human beings.

How you feel about this issue depends partly on when you think a new life is formed. Some people think that moment comes at the point an egg is fertilised (either by a sperm cell, or through the nucleus transfer described above). Perhaps, in this case, destroying embryos is no different to killing any human being. However, others believe it's a mistake to think of such a tiny bundle of cells as if it were a person. Stem cell research (although still in its early stages) has the potential to save the lives of people with painful and life-threatening diseases. Destroying embryos at such an early stage, many months before they develop any sort of feelings or sensations, is justified in order to reach that end.

Another, rather less convincing, reason for cloning has been put forward by an unusual group of people called the Raelians. They believe that cloning holds the key to everlasting life. They also claim to be pioneering the transfer of memories and experiences from one person to another. In this way a person's physical and mental characteristics could be zapped into a new body whenever the old one was nearing death. Although few scientists have much faith in Raelian experiments, their ideas raise some interesting questions about what makes us who we are. You can flick back to *Minds and Bodies* for a reminder of some of these.

Opening the floodgates

While many people would be pleased to see cloning used to cure disease, they're uncomfortable with the idea of living forever, or creating complete human beings. It's easy to believe that allowing one of these uses will open the floodgates to all the others. But perhaps this is just a slippery slope argument, like those we looked at in *Arguments (and how to win them!)*.

Science versus technology

We've seen that scientific discoveries can be put to good use and bad. Without science there'd have been no atomic bomb, but there'd also have been no painkillers, or cancer treatments. Perhaps science needs to be separated from the uses, or technologies, to which it's put. After all, aren't scientists merely seekers of truth? Aren't they interested purely in the way the world works?

We explored this idea at the beginning of the chapter and saw that scientists, like everyone else, have beliefs and opinions that affect the way they see the world. What's more, research institutions and professional journals may also influence the sorts of work that scientists conduct. For example, pharmaceuticals companies are interested in producing effective medicines, but they're also interested in making money. This has the potential to put pressure on scientists to deliver the results that the companies want to see.

The scientific community is also extremely competitive. A successful career usually depends on large numbers of publications, and this can drive people to write up their experiments before they've conducted all the necessary research. This problem can be made worse by the problem of publication bias. This is a tendency for scientific journals to publish positive results rather than negative ones. After all, most people would rather read about amazing discoveries than ideas that turned out to be wrong. If experiments carried out by two groups of scientists suggest different conclusions – one supporting a certain theory and one rejecting it – it may be that only the positive results get published. This can give the misleading impression that the theory has been proved.

Thanks to the usefulness of electricity and telephones and cars and fridges, people will always have much to thank science for. But we've also seen that the scientific process isn't quite as foolproof as we first thought. It's important to continue to question its methods and asked ourselves what, if anything, the limits of science should be. After all, science is practised by human beings, and human beings can be unreliable.

Puzzles and Paradoxes

In this chapter, we'll take a quick look at some of the biggest unsolved puzzles in philosophy. Many are known as **paradoxes**, and as any philosopher will tell you, these are the most fiendishly mind-bending problems of all.

In a paradox, a series of perfectly sensible steps seems to lead to an impossible conclusion. The following examples have perplexed philosophers for thousands of years. But even though in most cases you won't be able to find solutions, you should have fun trying …

Liar, liar

Imagine someone told you they always lied. If what they say is true, then they don't always lie at all. So what they say is false.

But if what they say is false, it looks like the person is a liar after all. So what they say is true.

Or, in other words:

- If the claim 'I always lie' is true, then it must be false.

- But if the claim 'I always lie' is false, then it must be true!

True or false?

Now take a look at the box below ...

THE SENTENCE BELOW IS TRUE
THE SENTENCE ABOVE IS FALSE

Is the top sentence true? If it is, then the bottom sentence must also be true. But the bottom sentence says that the top sentence is false!

So perhaps the top sentence *is* false. Then the bottom sentence must be false too. And if the bottom sentence is false it means the top sentence must be true after all!

Like many paradoxes, this puzzle seems simple at first, but the more you think about it, the more baffling it becomes!

★

Here's another paradox about the importance of revising for exams.

A testing problem

One dreary Monday morning, Mrs Patel tells her class to expect a surprise test one day that week. Miserably the class get down to work. All except Salma, who thinks she's spotted a flaw in her teacher's plan. Instead she spends the morning scratching rude poems into her desk with a compass.

'The thing is,' she explains to her best friend Katie, 'Mrs Patel said the test would be a surprise. That means it can't be on Friday.'

'Why not?' asks Katie. 'If it's a surprise, it could be any day.'

If we haven't had the test by the end of Thursday,' replies Salma, 'then we'd know it was going to be on Friday. And if we knew it was going to be on Friday, it wouldn't be a surprise at all.'

'OK,' replies Katie. 'So it won't be on Friday. It could still be any time between now and Thursday.'

'It can't be Thursday either,' continues Salma, 'because if we haven't had it by the end of Wednesday, and we know it can't be on Friday, then it would have to be on Thursday. And if it has to be on Thursday, that's not a surprise either.'

'And I suppose it can't be on Wednesday,' says Katie, 'because if we haven't had it by the end of Tuesday, and it can't be on Thursday or Friday, it would have to be on Wednesday. But it's not a surprise if we know when it has to be. It can't be

Tuesday for the same reasons. So it must be today.' Salma smiles. 'How could it be a surprise if we *knew* it was today?'

Katie smiles too. Salma must be right. The test can only be a surprise if it's unexpected. And since Mrs Patel won't be able to carry out her threat, there's no need to start revising.

Unfortunately, on Thursday afternoon (quite out of the blue) Mrs Patel announces the test. Salma and Katie were completely surprised after all!

Don't worry if you can't see where the friends went wrong. This paradox has left some of the greatest thinkers of all time scratching their heads in confusion. Why don't you try it out on your teacher, and see if it stumps them as well.

★

Lawyers have a reputation for being slippery customers. The following paradox might explain why.

A legal loophole

Zehra is desperate to become a lawyer but can't afford the price of the course. Luckily, her teacher suggests the following agreement: Zehra only has to pay him when she wins her first case.

Zehra's very excited, but after three years of gruelling training, she decides not to become a lawyer after all. And since she'll never win any cases now, she refuses to pay for her lessons. Unfortunately, her teacher is one of the cleverest lawyers in the country. He decides to take Zehra to court to force her to cough up.

As far as he's concerned, his plan can't fail. If he wins his case, the judge will force her to hand over what she owes. But even if Zehra wins she'll still have to pay. (According to the terms of the original agreement, she promised to pay when she won her first case.) Either way, the teacher will get his money!

But Zehra's not so sure. As she sees it, if she loses, she won't owe anything at all. (The original agreement says she only has to pay if she *wins* her first case.) On the other hand, if she *does* win, she'll still be in luck. The judge will dismiss the teacher's claim and she won't be made to pay a penny!

Zehra and her teacher can't both be right. But who do you think will end up out of pocket? (As you've probably guessed by now, this is another puzzle that seems to go round and round in circles.)

The world's fastest animal

The difficulty in getting from A to B is one of several paradoxes discovered by the Ancient Greek philosopher **Zeno of Elea**. Zeno's most famous example involves a race between the great athlete and warrior Achilles and a tortoise.

The tortoise, feeling at a serious disadvantage, asks for a head start. Achilles agrees and the signal is given for the contest to begin.

But although the tortoise is very slow indeed, Achilles tries in vain to win the race. After a few seconds he gets to the point at which the tortoise began, but his opponent has also moved on a small amount. In the time it takes Achilles to cover the extra distance, the tortoise has moved on again, and so on. According to Zeno, even if the race was to go on forever, Achilles would never quite catch up with the tortoise.

Of course, anyone who's gone to the trouble of

racing a tortoise will tell you just how easy it is to win. This is a classic paradox. Once again, all the steps of the argument appear to add up, but the conclusion is completely improbable.

The prisoners' dilemma

The following problem can be used to show that, when people work together, they produce the best results for everyone. But all too often, we pursue our own selfish interests.

★

The day after a bungled bank robbery, two suspects are immediately arrested – the well-known criminal 'Mongrel' McNeill and another shady character known as 'Chins'. As the men are taken to separate cells, McNeill hisses 'deny everything' at his accomplice.

Visiting them separately, the investigating officer offers both men the same deal. If they confess, he'll recommend two years each in prison. If only one man owns up, he'll reward his honesty by reducing his sentence to six months. But as an extra punishment, the other man will serve five years. If both men deny involvement, there won't be enough evidence to convict them of this crime. Instead they'll get a year each in prison on another minor charge.

It helps to see these options drawn up in a table.

	Chins owns up	**Chins denies everything**
McNeill owns up	Both men get two years	McNeill gets six months Chins gets five years
McNeill denies everything	McNeill gets five years Chins gets six months	Both men get one year

At first, McNeill isn't too worried. As long as both he and Chins plead innocence, they'll only spend a year each in prison. Then again, he muses, if Chins *does* deny everything, he could reduce his own sentence even further by owning up. That way he'll get away with a six-month term. (He isn't the least bit concerned that Chins' sentence would increase to five years.)

There's just one problem with the plan – Chins is every bit as villainous as his partner. He *also* realises he could reduce his sentence by owning up. Hopefully, McNeill will foolishly stick to the bargain himself, and Chins will get the shorter, six-month sentence.

Deviously, *both* men decide to own up. Unfortunately, this means they both get two years! (Look back to the table to see why.) If they'd stuck to their original deal, they'd only have got one year each. Instead, both acted selfishly to get the best outcome for themselves.

The 'Prisoners' Dilemma' shows the importance of sticking to your word, but often that's easier said than done. The problem with co-operating with other people is that it often seems at odds with what's best for us. Spending a year in prison is a lot worse than six months. But by both pursuing their own best interests, McNeill and Chins ended up with a very bad deal.

A philosophical poem

Some philosophers have approached their subject in a rather more lyrical way. This famous poem was written in the 19th century by an unknown author.

> Ten weary, footsore travellers,
> All in a woeful plight,
> Sought shelter at a wayside inn
> One dark and stormy night.

> 'Nine rooms, no more,' the landlord said
> 'Have I to offer you.
> To each of eight a single bed,
> But the ninth must serve for two.'

A din arose. The troubled host
Could only scratch his head,
For of those tired men not two
Would occupy one bed.

The puzzled host was soon at ease –
He was a clever man –
And so to please his guests devised
This most ingenious plan.

In a room marked A two men were placed,
The third was lodged in B,
The fourth to C was then assigned,
The fifth retired to D.

In E the sixth he tucked away,
In F the seventh man.
The eighth and ninth in G and H,
And then to A he ran,

Wherein the host, as I have said,
Had laid two travellers by;
Then taking one – the tenth and last –
He lodged him safe in I.

Nine single rooms – a room for each –
Were made to serve for ten;
And this it is that puzzles me
And many wiser men.

You might be relieved to hear that this problem actually does have a solution! To spot it, ask yourself if the tenth man really is the one who's been left in room A. Or is the landlord guilty of some sneaky double counting? (Top tip: what's going on becomes a lot clearer if you draw the rooms on a piece of paper.)

Some puzzles of infinity

Many problems in philosophy are concerned with space and time. In particular, people have often wondered if they both go on forever.

Things that go on forever are said to be **infinite**. On the other hand, if we know something's going to end we say that it's **finite**. A day is finite because it will end after 24 hours. Life might also be said to be finite, since plants and animals eventually die. (However, many people believe in a spiritual afterlife that does go on forever, as we saw in *God and Nature*.)

The idea of infinity lies at the heart of many philosophical puzzles. For example, imagine an infinitely long road – a road that goes on and on and never ends. If you lived forever, would you be able to walk its entire length?

The distance between the Earth and the moon is approximately 384,399 kilometres. But what is the distance between where you are sitting now and the edge of the universe? That depends on whether there even is an edge to the universe.

Do aliens exist?

Have you ever wondered if there might be life on other planets? No one has ever discovered proof of alien beings, but if the universe really is infinite, we can't rule out the possibility that they're out there somewhere.

To understand why, imagine flying a rocket towards the very edge of space. If the universe was infinite you'd never reach your destination, even if you were able to travel until the end of time. If, after a hundred years, you hadn't come across a single planet supporting life, you still couldn't say no such planet existed. Even after a million years of fruitless exploration, you couldn't know, for definite, that alien life forms didn't exist. In an infinite universe there's always the chance that new planets will be just around the corner.

★

Scientists have found many ways of travelling through space, but will we ever be able to travel through time? Might we be able to visit the past, or even glimpse the future?

The final paradox in this chapter is one of the most interesting and puzzling of all. Many philosophers think it shows why time travel will always remain an impossible dream.

The time travel paradox

World-famous physicist Dr Ghaffari has spent many months perfecting a time-travelling machine. But falling asleep at his desk one evening, he has an unsettling dream.

In his dream, Dr Ghaffari prepares to undertake his maiden voyage. He sets the coordinates for 50 years in the past and activates his specially modified nuclear reactor. The time machine rattles violently for a moment, there's a loud bang and then silence.

Cautiously, Dr Ghaffari opens the door. To his delight he sees he has indeed travelled back in time and materialised in the very village where his parents grew up. A small crowd has even gathered to witness his arrival.

But he can't help noticing that people don't seem very pleased to see him. There's lots of screaming going on and quite a few people are in tears. Dr Ghaffari reassures them that he's not an alien, but the villagers are far from impressed. A vaguely familiar man approaches Dr Ghaffari and says,

'I don't care where you're from, your stupid contraption has landed on my son!'

Dr Ghaffari is horrified, but looking back over his shoulder he can see two small feet poking out from under his glistening machine.

'What was the poor boy's name?' he stammers, unable to believe his eyes.

'That was little Amir Ghaffari,' says one of the other villagers. 'He was the most intelligent child in the village and now he's as flat as a pancake.'

'B ... but that's impossible,' Dr Ghaffari protests. 'Amir is my father's name. I am Amir Ghaffari's son.'

'Don't be ridiculous,' says the first man, who the doctor realises must be his grandfather. 'Little Amir's not going to have any children is he? He's just been squashed by a flying saucer.'

Dr Ghaffari wakes up in a cold sweat, his grandfather's words ringing in his ears and his hopes of time travel in tatters.

It's all in the stars

Dr Ghaffari's nightmare shows why this type of time travel is impossible. If Amir had been killed when he was a boy, the doctor would never have been born. But if he'd never been born, he couldn't have invented the machine that squashed his own father.

Despite this paradox, scientists haven't given up on the idea of time travel altogether. Although it may be impossible for very large objects like human beings to go back in time, the same might not be true of very tiny particles, especially if they were sucked into a Black Hole.

Most scientists believe that Black Holes begin their lives as gigantic stars, or super-novae, many times bigger and heavier than our own sun. Like all stars, supernovae are fiercely burning balls of gas. When that gas is burnt up, they 'die' and collapse in on themselves. The crush is so intense that not even light can escape – which is why nobody has ever actually seen one.

Inside Black Holes, the pressure is so great that scientists think the normal laws of physics get bent out of shape. No one's really sure what goes on at their core, but one possibility is that microscopic passage-ways, known as worm-holes, are created. These tunnel-like structures may provide paths from one time period to another.

Although you can't see Black Holes, you can experience a kind of time travel just by looking up at the stars on a cloudless night. The light they emit has taken thousands, or even millions, of years to travel across space. Some of these stars may no longer actually exist. What we see is what they looked like in the past, at the moment when the starlight started crossing space towards us.

With the aid of powerful telescopes, astronomers have been able to see galaxies more than 10 billion light years away. (In other words, the light has taken 10 billion years to reach us.) Scientists think that earth is roughly 5 billion years old. Through these telescopes it's possible to see what a star looked like long before our planet even existed!

Big Thinkers

Throughout this book we've rubbed shoulders with some of the most influential thinkers of all time. Here's a bit more information about ten of the best ...

1. Zeno of Elea

Born: Greece

Lived: 490–425 BCE

Big ideas: Zeno, one of the earliest of the Ancient Greek philosophers, is best known for his **paradoxes**: he was responsible for the example about Achilles and the tortoise, which we saw in *Puzzles and Paradoxes*. In total, Zeno devised over 40 similar problems, including one about the difficulty in getting from here to there. That argument goes something like this:

Imagine the place you want to get to is exactly a mile away. To reach your destination you'd have to pass the half-way point first. (In other words, you'd have to travel half the distance before you could travel the whole distance.) But before you reach that half-way point, you'd have to travel half *that* distance too (a quarter of the total distance). What's more, you couldn't get a quarter of the way until you'd travelled an eighth of the distance, and so on. The problem is, each of these little distances will take a certain amount of time to travel. And since you can keep dividing the distance into smaller and smaller fractions forever (1/16, 1/32, 1/64, etc.), you'll always be adding to the time it takes to complete your journey. According to Zeno, it will actually take an **infinite** amount of time to reach your destination!

Luckily, most of us manage to get where we need to in a **finite**, rather than an infinite, amount of time. But it's very difficult to see what's wrong with Zeno's argument.

Lesser-known facts: Very little is actually known about Zeno. Most of the information we have comes from the writings of Plato. A few other details were recorded by the Greek author Diogenes Laertius. According to him, Zeno tried single-handedly to overturn the tyrannical ruler of Elea where he was born. Unfortunately, there isn't any other evidence of such heroic bravery. Laertius probably let his imagination run away with him.

2. Plato

Born: Greece

Lived: 427–347 BCE

Big ideas: Plato is probably the most famous philosopher of all time, partly because he introduced the world to another brilliant thinker, Socrates. Socrates was an inspirational teacher to Plato and many others, but the Greek authorities were convinced his ideas were corrupting the young people of Athens. In 399 BCE they sentenced him to death by forcing him to drink the poison hemlock.

Socrates never recorded any of his own ideas, but Plato wrote a number of books in which his old teacher is shown debating with others. In these writings, Plato touches on a huge range of subjects from politics and religion to ethics, love and the role of women. In 'The Republic' (Plato's most famous work), he argues that men and women should have equal access to education, a view that was well ahead of its time. Plato attached huge importance to education and in 387 BCE he opened his own 'Academy' dedicated to teaching philosophical ideas.

Elsewhere in the *The Republic*, Plato suggests how a perfect state should be split into three levels. At the top, wise philosopher-kings would govern on behalf of the whole society. (Plato distrusted any form of democracy, believing that only those of the highest intelligence could know which decisions were for the best.) The second level would consist of soldiers and civil servants, and beneath them would be a class of workers generating society's wealth. Plato stresses that everyone must accept their role and not seek to move to a different level.

Lesser-known facts: Plato had little time for artists and poets, who he felt misrepresented the truth about the world. Rather than trying to show things as they actually were, they created pale imitations of reality. In his republic, only a very few artists, authorised by the philosopher-kings, would be allowed.

3. Aristotle

Born: Greece

Lived: 384–322 BCE

Big ideas: Aristotle began his career as the star pupil at Plato's school for philosophers. And for the rest of his life he remained fascinated by the natural world, writing on subjects including astronomy, biology, geography, anatomy and physics. He believed passionately that the secrets of the universe could be uncovered by observation and experiment. Many of the ideas about the **scientific method** that we looked at in *Science and Scientists* owe their origin to Aristotle.

Aristotle also explored questions of right and wrong and suggested ways to help achieve fulfilment in life. (Not surprisingly, these involved spending a lot of time thinking and reading books.)

Turning his attention to the nature of art and literature, he identified the importance of having a beginning, middle and end in storytelling. And on his days off he developed a system of logic, elements of which are still in use today. For example, Aristotle was responsible for the idea of the **syllogism**, which we looked at in *Arguments (and how to win them!)*.

In 343 BCE, King Philip of Macedonia asked Aristotle to tutor his thirteen-year-old heir, Alexander. Alexander the Great (as he later became known) proved extremely good at winning arguments, although in this case through force. By the time of his death he had conquered much of the known world.

Aristotle returned to Athens in 335 BCE and founded a school of his own. The Lyceum became a rival to Plato's Academy (although Plato himself had died over ten years before).

Lesser-known facts: Aristotle's ideas had a considerable influence on the development of Islamic thinking. In the 9th and 10th centuries in particular, Arab scholars studied and preserved the works of many ancient Greek philosophers. Later these writings were reintroduced into European countries that might otherwise have lost them forever.

In some other respects, Aristotle's reputation as a brilliant thinker restricted the growth of new ideas. For a long time he was known simply as 'The Philosopher', and anyone who dared to criticise his ideas was treated with suspicion. It wasn't until the 17th century that philosophy began to emerge from his shadow, as we'll see in a moment ...

4. Descartes

Born: France

Lived: 1596–1650

Big ideas: Descartes is often described as the first philosopher of modern times. The 17th century may not seem very modern these days, but it did mark a turning point in how people thought about the world.

Up until then, most of what people understood about the world came from reading books. Few people questioned what was written, particularly if the author was a respectable ancient philosopher like Aristotle. However, early in his life, Descartes decided not to take anything for granted. He decided to look at the world through fresh eyes, refusing to simply accept what he'd read or been told.

Descartes began by asking himself what he really knew, and soon he became convinced that wasn't very much. He realised that our senses (sight, sound, touch, taste and smell) often mislead us. He even wondered if the world around us was no more real than the places we visit in our dreams.

But eventually Descartes had a breakthrough and discovered something he thought he knew for sure. Even if trees and mountains didn't exist, even if his own body didn't exist, even if everything he thought he knew was mistaken, there must still be a 'him' making these mistakes. He could doubt all sorts of things, but he couldn't doubt the existence of his own mind.

In *Minds and Bodies*, we saw some of the problems that follow from Descartes' big idea. But whether we agree with him or not, his decision to doubt and question everything has inspired thinkers ever since.

Lesser-known facts: Descartes spent his life trying to understand how minds and bodies interact with each other. In the end, he thought that a little part of the brain, called the pineal gland (which we now know helps control our body clocks) was where this kind of activity went on. Descartes believed the pineal gland was the home of the human soul.

5. David Hume

Born: Scotland

Lived: 1711–1776

Big ideas: You might remember David Hume from the *Science and Scientists* chapter. He was the philosopher who first suggested that one day the sun might stop rising in the morning. This rather shocking idea was the result of his belief that we only come to know things through direct experience of the outside world. This idea was very new to philosophy at the time. Previous thinkers, as we saw with Descartes, had argued that we can discover many truths about the universe (like whether or not God exists) simply by the power of thought, or reason. But Hume was convinced that knowledge comes to us through our five senses alone. He also believed that although our senses give us knowledge of what objects look like, sound like etc., they can't give us knowledge of how different experiences are linked.

For instance, whenever you kick a ball, the ball will move. And since this relationship between kicking a ball and it moving has always been there in the past, we expect it will be there in the future too. In other words, we *assume* that kicking a ball will always *cause* it to move. We expect that these two experiences will always be linked in this way. The problem for Hume is that this expectation relies on the assumption that the future must actually be like the past. And as Anna showed in *Science and Scientists*, that assumption isn't as reliable as we might think.

Lesser-known facts: Fortunately for his sanity, David Hume didn't spend all his life worrying about the future. He also spent a great deal of time thinking about the past, and his *History of Great Britain* was the standard history text book for much of the 18th century. He was also fascinated by the philosophy of religion but, since he didn't appear to believe in God, his views often got him into trouble. Contradicting the established religious views of the time could land you in prison – a fate that Hume only narrowly avoided. However, he was turned down for many high profile jobs because of his unpopular views.

6. Immanuel Kant

Born: Germany

Lived: 1724–1804

Big ideas: Immanuel Kant once wrote that there were two things that filled him with wonder and curiosity – 'the starry sky above me, and the moral law within me'. And sure enough, these were the two areas of philosophy that preoccupied him throughout his life. In 1781 he published an enormous book all about the universe and what we actually know about it, and in 1788 he wrote another massive volume all about right and wrong. On this subject Kant was very clear. He believed that (in any given situation) you should do something only if you'd be happy for anyone else in that situation to do the same. (We looked at this idea in *Right and Wrong*.)

But Kant is even more famous for his ideas about how we learn about the outside world. He believed that there's a difference between the world *as it appears to us*, and the world *as it really is*. He argued that the information we get through our five senses is arranged in certain ways by our minds. The way we see an object is therefore the result of two things – what the object is really like, and the particular way our own minds are constructed. What's more, since we can't experience anything without our minds, we will *never* see the world as it really is. This kind of knowledge is simply impossible for human beings to have.

Kant named his philosophy after Nicolaus Copernicus, the scientist who first showed that the Earth travelled round the sun rather than the other way around (an idea we looked at in *Science and Scientists*). Kant believed that his own 'Copernican revolution' had turned philosophy's search for knowledge on its head. He showed that there were limits to what we can know about the world around us.

Lesser-known facts: Kant was probably the most punctual philosopher who ever lived. He was never late for appointments, and always took his daily walk to church at exactly the same time. In fact, he was so reliable his neighbours used to set their clocks by him. On one occasion, however, he found himself completely absorbed by a book by another great thinker, Jean Jacques Rousseau. He missed church for several days, leaving his fellow villagers extremely confused!

7. John Stuart Mill

Born: England

Lived: 1806–1873

Big ideas: As a child, John Stuart Mill was exceptionally clever. He began learning Ancient Greek at the age of just three and pretty soon moved on to Latin. As a teenager he turned his attention to philosophy and economics, quickly cracking them as well.

With such a powerful brain, it's not surprising he developed some of the most influential ideas in the philosophy of ethics – the study of right and wrong. Most famously, he believed that the right thing to do in any situation was whatever was likely to bring the greatest happiness to the largest number of people. In other words, you'd be able to judge if an action, or decision, was right by working out how much it would benefit people's lives. (This is an argument we looked at in *Right and Wrong*. It's sometimes called a consequentialist philosophy, because it's concerned with the consequences of people's actions.)

Mill was also interested in social reform and caused controversy in his lifetime by championing the rights of women. In the 19th century, women were denied the right to vote and in many cases they were barred from education and employment as well. Mill argued that there was no good reason why women shouldn't enjoy the same opportunities as men. In 1867 he even helped to form one of the first organisations dedicated to getting women the vote (The London Society for

Women's Suffrage). But despite his efforts, this goal wasn't achieved for a further 50 years. Women were finally allowed to vote in 1918, as long as they were over 30. In 1928 the voting age was lowered to 21 – the same age as for men at the time.

Lesser-known facts: Mill adapted many of his ideas from his teacher and godfather Jeremy Bentham (1748–1832). Bentham asked that when he died his body should be mummified and exhibited at the new University College London (now part of London University). Unfortunately, the mummification process didn't go according to plan and Bentham's head was badly damaged. However, you can still see the rest of his body (complete with new wax head) displayed in UCL's main building in Gower Street in London! (http://www.ucl.ac.uk)

8. Charles Darwin

Born: England

Lived: 1809–1882

Big ideas: From an early age, Charles Darwin was fascinated with the natural world, collecting and studying plants and wildlife whenever he could. Although he didn't do particularly well at school, he hoped to become a doctor and went to university in Scotland to study medicine. However, the experience of watching a gruesome operation performed on a young boy without anaesthetic proved too much for him. He abandoned his studies and moved to Cambridge to study theology instead. After university, he was given a surprise opportunity to travel the world, working as an unpaid naturalist on the ship HMS *Beagle*. The experience was to change his life forever.

Before he left, Darwin had become interested in the ideas of the geologist Charles Lyell. Lyell believed that fossils were the remains of animals that had lived thousands, maybe millions, of years ago. On the voyage, Darwin made detailed notes on the many new fossils he and the crew discovered as well as the hundreds of never-seen-before animals and plants. Some of the most incredible discoveries were made when the ship reached the Galapagos Islands off the coast of South America in the Pacific Ocean. In particular, Darwin discovered several varieties of finches scattered across the different islands. Some had short beaks useful for eating seeds, while others had longer beaks more suited to catching insects.

Darwin didn't realise the significance of these birds at first, but following his return to England he realised that the different varieties had adapted to cope with the particular environments of their different islands. This discovery helped Darwin develop his groundbreaking theory of **natural selection**.

Darwin spent 20 years refining his ideas and collecting a mass of fossil evidence before eventually publishing *The Origin of Species* in 1859. (The timing was partly due to his worry that another scientist, Alfred Russel Wallace, who had been working along very similar lines, might be about to steal his thunder.) In the book, Darwin explained how the offspring of particular species always show considerable variation. He went on to argue that it is the offspring most suited to their environment that will survive. It will be their characteristics, therefore, that are passed to the next generation.

As we saw in *God and Nature*, Darwin's ideas caused fierce controversy. The established Church felt this new **theory of evolution** threatened their teachings. However, *The Origin of Species* captured the public's imagination. The first print-run of the book sold out on the very day it was published.

Lesser-known facts: Although Darwin's theory is often referred to as 'the survival of the fittest', this expression didn't appear anywhere in the original edition of *The Origin of Species*. However, he did insert it into the fifth edition published in 1869. (As we saw in *God and Nature*, survival of the fittest doesn't just mean survival of the strongest. Instead, it means the survival of those that are best adapted to their particular environment.)

9. Bertrand Russell

Born: England

Lived: 1872–1970

Big ideas: The life of Bertrand Russell is proof that philosophy can drive the cleverest people round the twist. We've seen that philosophical puzzles can be intriguing and perplexing (see *Puzzles and Paradoxes*), but at the beginning of the 20th century, this particular example (about a barber who shaves people's beards) brought Russell to the brink of despair:

If the town barber shaves only those people who don't shave themselves, who shaves the barber?

The problem is, the barber can't shave himself, because he shaves *only* those people who *don't* shave themselves. Then again, if he doesn't shave himself, he's just the sort of person he *would* shave.

Russell had been exploring groups, or sets, of objects. He believed that everything belonged to at least one set. For example, cats and dogs belong to the set of animals, triangles and squares belong to the set of shapes, etc. Curiously, some sets can even be members of themselves. For example, the set of all sets is, itself, a set.

With his discovery of the barber's paradox, however, Russell discovered a set that didn't fit this pattern – the set of all sets that are *not* members of themselves. This set can't be a member of itself, because it contains only those sets that are *not* members of themselves. But if the set is not a member of itself, it *would* be one of its own members. (You'll probably need to read back over that a few times before it starts to make sense!)

This mind-bending realisation shattered Russell's belief in the purity of logic and mathematics.

Lesser-known facts: Bertrand Russell was the grandson of a former prime minister, and was active in politics throughout his life. A pacifist during the First World

War, he spent six months in prison in 1918 for his out-spoken views. He was also a champion of women's rights and later the president of the Campaign for Nuclear Disarmament (CND).

Russell was also extremely fond of smoking pipes, a fact that saved his life in 1948. In November of that year he was involved in a plane crash on the way to present a lecture in Norway. All the people in the non-smoking compartment were killed.

10. Ludwig Wittgenstein

Born: Austria

Lived: 1889–1951

Big ideas: The philosophy of Ludwig Wittgenstein is particularly hard to summarise. Throughout his life he was fascinated by the way that language relates to the real world. For example, what does the word 'red' actually mean? Does it refer to something that exists in the universe? Or does its meaning come from the ways in which we use it – a red bus, a red flower, a red-letter day etc.

As we saw in *Art and Artists*, Wittgenstein was puzzled by how to define things. Take the word 'game', which can apply to all sorts of objects and activities – a card game, a game of squash, a game of chess. It's very difficult to find something that all games have in common, but that doesn't prove we don't know what the word really *means*. Wittgenstein thought the different meanings of words were rather like members of the same family. There isn't necessarily one single characteristic that everyone in the family shares (a big nose, for example). However, it's possible to see lots of little similarities and recognise that everyone's related. Wittgenstein applied some of these ideas to the question 'what is art?' (See *Art and Artists*.)

Lesser-known facts: Wittgenstein was a restless figure who witnessed many tragedies in his life. He was one of eight children born into an extremely wealthy Austrian family. However, three of his four brothers committed suicide. Wittgenstein also saw terrible suffering during the First World War when he was a solider in the Austrian Army. His first book, *The Tractatus* (written in the trenches), was full of very precise and ordered thoughts. This may have been a reaction to the chaos all around him. Despite studying at Cambridge before the war, when it was over he travelled to a small Austrian village to become a school teacher. But he eventually returned to both England and philosophy.

Final Words

In the introduction to this book, we learned a bit about Socrates, possibly the greatest philosopher of all time. Although he was executed by the Athenian state, he had lived until 70 – an old age by the standards of the time. Throughout his long life, he had thought deeply about many of the questions we've explored in these chapters. And yet, he surprised his followers by declaring, 'All I know is that I know nothing.'

Socrates wasn't just being modest. And he certainly didn't believe he was stupid either. However, he did understand how easy it is to accept things as true without really questioning them for ourselves. He realised that much of what we think we know is based on assumptions and the opinions of others.

Asking questions was what Socrates cared about more than anything. His words were a challenge to future thinkers – people like us. Even from beyond the grave, he continues to inspire people to examine the unanswered mysteries and puzzles of the universe.

Glossary

Analytic statements Statements that you know are true just by looking at them. For instance, 'All stripy tigers have stripes.' Even if you'd never seen a tiger before in your life, you'd know this statement *has* to be true.

Artificial intelligence The branch of science studied by people interested in whether machines could ever think like human beings.

Asexual reproduction The process by which some living things produce cells that develop into new offspring *by themselves*. The cells don't need to be fertilised by another member of the species.

Cause and effect The idea that anything that happens in the universe is the result of something happening before it.

Circular argument A very slippery argument in which what is being proved relies on us already accepting the answer we are looking for.

Cloning The process of making an identical genetic copy of another living thing.

Constituency A particular area of the country that is represented by a single member of parliament. The UK is split into 646 constituencies, which is why there are currently 646 MPs in the House of Commons.

Contract An agreement between two or more people. If a contract is between a government and its citizens, breaking it is almost always illegal.

Creationism The belief that the universe was *created* by God, or another higher being.

Democracy A form of government in which every citizen has an equal right to vote in an election. In practice, there are usually restrictions. In the UK, for example, people cannot vote until they are 18.

Determinism The idea that whatever happens in the universe is the result of everything that has happened before it. It relies on a belief in cause and effect, and suggests that we may not have any choice over our actions.

Dictatorship A system of government that means a country is ruled by a single person. Citizens do not have any say in decisions that affect them.

DNA The combination of chemicals that genes are made of.

Ethics Moral beliefs about right and wrong.

Ethical dilemma A difficult choice faced by people trying to decide how to do the right thing. Often, the different options will all have some advantages and disadvantages.

Finite Something is finite if it has fixed boundaries. For example, a day is finite because it always has 24 hours. A piece of string has a finite length because it doesn't go on forever.

Fundamentalists People who believe that particular ideas, often written down in religious texts like the Bible, are literally true.

Genes These can be thought of as a recipe book for our bodies. They are responsible for many characteristics, such as eye and skin colour, and are passed on from parents to their offspring.

Genetic engineering The changing of a plant's or animal's genetic make-up by artificial means.

Idealism The belief that there is no physical matter in the universe and that nothing is real except for our minds. (Idealism can also mean a belief that things might one day be perfect.)

Infinite Something is infinite if it goes on forever. For instance, numbers are infinite, because they never run out. However big a number you think of, you can always add 1 to it.

Intelligent design The idea that the universe is too amazing to have happened by chance. People who support this idea think the world must have been made deliberately, by God or some other higher being.

Materialism The belief that everything in the universe is made of physical matter. Even thoughts and emotions are just the result of physical processes (like chemical reactions).

Natural selection The process by which those organisms best adapted to their environment live longest and reproduce the most. They then pass on their successful characteristics to their offspring. The organisms less suited to their environment will die out.

Objectivity An important requirement for scientists and other thinkers. An idea is objective if it is based *only* on the facts and not prejudices or personal opinions.

Ontological argument An argument for the existence of God first put forward almost 1,000 years ago by a monk called Anselm.

Paradox A paradox is a series of apparently reasonable statements that seem to lead to an impossible conclusion.

Proportional representation This term applies to several different forms of voting. They all share the idea that the number of seats a political party gets in an election should reflect the number of people who voted for it.

Reproductive cloning Where human beings are concerned, this is a type of cloning that involves creating an embryo that will develop into a fully formed person.

Sceptic Someone who doubts everything.

Scientific method The way to describe the steps scientists take to develop theories. These involve observation, testing and making predictions about the future.

Sexual reproduction In this form of reproduction, two members of a species are always required. Each contributes half the genetic material needed to produce a new offspring.

Solipsism The belief that nothing actually exists outside of your mind. Your friends, your family, where you live etc. are all just figments of your imagination!

Statement A sentence that says something is the case. For example, '70 per cent of the earth's surface is covered by water.'

Syllogism A famous type of philosophical argument in which a particular conclusion follows on naturally from several other steps.

Theory of evolution The idea that species develop through the process of natural section. This theory was first proposed by Charles Darwin in his book *The Origin of Species* (1859).

Therapeutic cloning Where humans are concerned, this is a type of cloning that involves creating an embryo that will not be allowed to grow into a fully formed person. Instead the embryo will be used to collect cells that can be used in medical treatment, before being destroyed.

Thought experiment An imaginary situation designed to test philosophical ideas. Often they can identify hidden beliefs and assumptions, as the 'Runaway Train' example showed in *Right and Wrong*. They also help us to explore intriguing problems such as time travel, as we saw in *Puzzles and Paradoxes*.

Big Numbers: A mind-expanding trip to infinity and back

Mary and John Gribbin
Illustrated by
Ralph Edney and
Nicholas Halliday

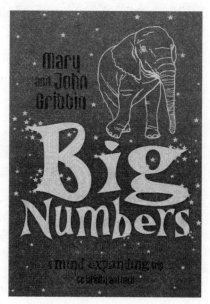

How big is infinity? How small is an electron?

When will the Sun destroy the Earth?

How fast is a nerve impulse in your brain?

Why can't you see inside a black hole?

What's the hottest temperature ever recorded on Earth?

What's the furthest you can see on a clear night?

Welcome to the amazing world of 'Big Numbers', where you'll travel from the furthest reaches of the known Universe to the tiniest particles that make up life on Earth. Together with Mary and John Gribbin, you can find out how our telescopes can see 10 billion years into the past, and why a thimbleful of a neutron star would contain as much mass as all the people on Earth put together!

UK £4.99 • Canada $10.00 • ISBN 1 84046 661 8

How to Remember (Almost) Everything, Ever!

Weird, isn't it? You can remember the name of every person in your favourite team or pop group, but you forget what day it is. Why is that? How does memory work and how can you can you make yours be the best?

Crammed with cool tricks, experiments and great mind games, this book can help you train your brain – amazing your friends AND impressing your teachers!

See the human mind take on the world's most powerful computer, discover how to make and break secret spy codes, and read incredible true-life memory stories about mighty Roman generals, daring prison escapes, and the amazing Russian man who could remember absolutely everything – ever!

UK £5.99 • Canada $12.00 • ISBN 1 84046 797 5